T-62s on the move in Afghanistan. Redeployment of forces to bases just inside the USSR has led to a drop in the Soviet troop level since 1980.
Tass

SOVIET LAND POWER

MARK L. URBAN

Great postwar changes in Military Doctrine resulted from the advent of nuclear weapons. Under Krushchev Russia's nuclear forces were built up at the expense of its conventional ones during the early 1960s. *Novosti*

SOVIET LAND POWER
MARK L. URBAN

IA
LONDON
IAN ALLAN LTD

CONTENTS

Siberian MD. *Novosti*

*To
my parents*

First published 1985

ISBN 0 7110 1442 6

Published by Ian Allan Ltd, Shepperton, Surrey;
and printed by Ian Allan Printing Ltd at their works
at Coombelands in Runnymede, England.

As this book went to press the death of Marshal Ustinov was
announced. He has been replaced by his First Deputy, Marshal
Sergei Sokolov. It has not been possible to make alterations to
this effect in the text. It remains to be seen whether Sokolov
will assume all of Ustinov's responsibilities, or whether, as
many analysts have suggested, the appointment of the 73-year
old Marshal is a stop gap measure.

It has been a conscious decision to
include in this volume photographs of
important interest, which might in
other conditions have been excluded
on grounds of quality. It is hoped that the
reader will accept the consequent reduction
in the production standards of some plates.

PREFACE

Since the war governments, academics and private industries have devoted huge resources to the study of Soviet military potential. Indirectly at least the West's intelligence agencies — particularly those in the USA — are the principal source of information on the subject. They have developed the timely leak to a fine art. A case in point were the allegations that the Soviets had used chemical weapons in Afghanistan and Cambodia which were timed to coincide with a debate in Congress on new chemical weapons for the American Army. For obvious reasons these intelligence disclosures rarely point to weaknesses or limitations in the Soviet Army. Whilst it is understandable that it should want to publicise those developments which concern it most, the Western intelligence community has been responsible for many examples of what might be called creative intelligence. Under political pressure to produce ever more disturbing revelations about Soviet military power it has allowed intelligence fact to be reshaped into political fiction.

Among the most infamous examples of creative intelligence were the bomber gap and missile gap scares of the 1950s and early 1960s. In both cases flimsy evidence was exaggerated to justify new programmes by the Pentagon. Recent US disclosures have been packaged slickly in a series of pamphlets called *Soviet Military Power*. These have contained many important new facts but also a measure of fiction. The first pamphlet for example had a picture of a revolutionary new tank designated T-80, but subsequent issues have carried photographs of a modified T-72, bearing no resemblance to the original, but having the same name — T-80. Whilst the bulk of the disclosures are sound and factual, these continued examples of 'threat inflation' mean that the independent observer must treat each new report with a degree of scepticism.

The Soviets' own publications cast light on some areas — particularly doctrine, history and training — and some shortcomings are even admitted in the letters column of *Red Star*. They are less forthcoming on subjects such as organisation and deployment, although occasional disclosures provide a means of verifying Western reports.

In compiling this book I have tried to consult as many sources as possible. In addition to these published reports I have also had the benefit of unofficial briefings from government analysts inside and outside NATO countries. Former members of the Soviet Army, and others who have seen it in action, have also provided me with much useful information. The result is, I hope, an objective analysis of Soviet Land Power examining its organisation, deployment, command and efficiency.

My thanks go to Bob Downey for the line illustrations, Cath Abraham, Chris Donnelly, Bob Elliot, Chris Foss, Sandy Gall, David Isby, Nigel Ryan and Chris Schneider, and to the librarians at the International Institute of Strategic Studies, Soviet Studies Centre Sandhurst, Imperial War Museum and Royal Geographical Society.

Mark L. Urban
1 January 1984

ABBREVIATIONS

Amphib	Amphibious			Military Operations
APC	Armoured Personnel Carrier		HEAT	High Explosive Anti-Tank
Arty	Artillery		HVAPFSDS	High Velocity Armour
Asslt	Assault			Piercing Fin Stabilised
ATGW	Anti-Tank Guided Weapon			Discarding Sabot
Bde	Brigade		KGB	*Komitet Gosudarstvenoy*
BK	*Boevoy Komplekt* — Unit of Fire			*Bezopasnosti* — Committee
BMD	*Boyevaya Mashina*			for State Security
	Desantnika — Airborne		KT	Kiloton
	Combat Vehicle		MD	Military District
BMP	*Boyevaya Mashina Pekhoty*		MPA	Main Political Administration
	— Infantry Fighting Vehicle		MR	Motor Rifle
BTR	*Bronetransporter* —		MTVD	*Moreskoi Teatr Voyennykh*
	Armoured Transporter			*Destviy* — Sea Theatre of
cat	Category of readiness			Military Operations
CBR	Chemical, Bacteriological,		MVD	Ministry of Internal Affairs
	and Radiation		NATO	North Atlantic Treaty
CIA	Central Intelligence Agency			Organisation
	(American)		NORTHAG	Northern Army Group (NATO)
C-in-C	Commander-in-Chief		NGF	Northern Group of Forces
CGF	Central Group of Forces		NSWP	Non-Soviet Warsaw Pact
COMSEC	Communications Security		OMG	Operational Manoeuvre Group
CPSU	Communist Party of the		OTVD	*Okeanski Teatr Voyennykh*
	Soviet Union			*Destviy* — Ocean Theatre of
CSSR	Czechoslovak Socialist Republic			Military Operations
Div	Division		PDP	People's Democratic Party
DOSAAF	*Dobrovolnoe Obshchestvo*			(of Afghanistan)
	Sodeistviya Armiy, Aviatsiy i		PVO	*Protivo-Vozdushnaya*
	Flota — Voluntary Society			*Oborona* — Air Defence, the
	for Co-operation with the			Voisk PVO are the Air
	Army, Air Force and Fleet			Defence Forces
DRA	Democratic Republic of		SGF	Southern Group of Forces
	Afghanistan		SIGINT	Signals Intelligence
ELINT	Electronic Intelligence		TEL	Transporter Erector
GDR	German Democratic Republic			Launcher (vehicle)
Gds	Guards		Tk	Tank
GRU	*Glavnoye Razvedyvatelnoye*		TVD	*Teatr Voyennykh Destviy* —
	Upravleniye — Main			Theatre of Military
	Intelligence Directorate of the			Operations
	General Staff		VDV	*Vozdushno Desantniki Voisk*
GSFG	Group of Soviet Forces in			— Air Assault Forces
	Germany		VTA	*Voyenno Transportnaya*
GTVD	*Glavny Teatr Voyennykh*			*Aviatsiya* — Military
	Destviy — Main Theatre of			Transport Aviation

1. THE MOTHERLAND CALLS

★

THE SOVIET WAY OF WAR

Whether we regard war as the continuation or the failure of politics the Soviet Army and Navy are the instruments of a particular political system. The officially accepted political view of war in the USSR is termed Military Doctrine. The ideas on war and peace as represented by Military Doctrine are a mixture of ideology, geography, history and military capability. Each of these elements is interconnected, so although we shall concentrate on military capability a superficial examination of the ideological, economic, geographical and historical influences on Soviet Military Doctrine is essential.

Ideologically speaking the USSR is theoretically incapable of starting a war. Marxism-Leninism holds that states may be distinguished from one another by their class character. The USSR and its socialist allies represent the progressive bloc, ruled by a peace-loving dictatorship of the working class. The USA and western European states on the other hand represent the forces of imperialism and reaction anxious to check the advance of progressive (ie Soviet) mankind, and are constantly at war with one another. Marxism teaches that capitalism (of which imperialism is the highest form) and socialism are engaged in a constant struggle, the outcome of which can only be the victory of socialism. Lenin decided, and subsequent Soviet leaders have accepted, that the current era is one of peaceful coexistence in which socialist and imperialist states are living side by side. Peaceful coexistence does not however rule out Soviet assistance to communist elements within the imperialist or developing states,

nor does it safeguard these states from the 'objective process of history' (ie the decline of capitalism and the advance of socialism). The importance of ideology in Soviet security policy is tempered in a number of ways.

The first is the tendency to see the interests of world socialism as being identical with the interests of the leading socialist state, ie the USSR. The second is the fact that the Communist Party of the Soviet Union (CPSU) reserves the right to develop its ideology, and this is important in the light of developments such as nuclear weapons. Lastly, a sufficiently talented ideologue, of which there are many in the East, can find within the collected works of Marx, Engels and Lenin a justification for just about any course of foreign policy the Kremlin wishes to take. The importance of ideology in current Soviet Military Doctrine lies in the fact that it unites the leadership in a common overall view of global security and gives scholarly and 'scientific' substance to policy.

In any Western view of Soviet military potential we must assume that the men in the Kremlin have a rational view of war and peace. Russia lost 20million people last time there was a world war, and who knows how many would die in a nuclear conflict. P. H. Vigor, formerly head of the Soviet Studies Centre at Sandhurst, stated that as long as the West maintains a nuclear deterrent 'one can be quite sure that it will be the policy of the Soviet leaders not to engage in nuclear war if they can possibly avoid it; nor to engage in a war of conventional weapons that is likely to escalate further'. As the former Soviet leader Leonid Brezhnev stated in October 1981, 'Anybody's decision to start a nuclear war in the hope of winning it is tantamount to suicide'. The Soviet leadership well understands that in a global nuclear war the states with the largest population and greatest economy would stand the best chance of survival. A study of the world today tells it that the West still has a better chance than the East: this is the reality behind the doctrine of peaceful coexistence. It is also the reality which leads the Soviet Union to act in international affairs on the basis of cautious pragmatism. The sending Soviet troops into Czechoslovakia in 1968 or Afghanistan in 1979 should be seen as attempts to secure the borders of the USSR and not as evidence of some grand design of global domination. Anybody who believes that these actions *are* part of a scheme of global domination would be advised to look at the record of other superpowers laying waste to whole countries thousands of miles from their own borders: Soviet security policy has yet to produce a Vietnam. The fact that Soviet security policy has produced fewer invasions than those of other superpowers, and that the Soviets have only intervened in countries on their own borders, does not necessarily make this policy right, for after all Soviet communists claim their foreign policy to be the result of some 'scientific' ideology. The CPSU rules by a dictatorship of the proletariat, and a study of the means used within the USSR to maintain

the Party's monopoly of power shows that it is often prepared to use coercive methods, and violate human rights. But there is no way that the West can force the USSR to change its internal policies and attempts to do so by sanctions and embargoes have been expensive failures. In an age of strategic nuclear weapons it is a dangerous fantasy to suppose that the West could roll back the dictatorship of the proletariat in the USSR, Poland or any other eastern European states. Stability and perhaps survival demand the treatment of the USSR as an equal partner in international affairs with a right to peace and security.

Today the superpowers have accelerated the build-up and modernisation of their forces, and in this climate of tension the Soviets are usually cast in the role of aggressor. But it takes two to make an arms race, and Western technology has usually made the running: the atom bomb, supersonic jet fighters, missile launching submarines and many other systems were all developed and fielded by the West some years before they were by the USSR. Western calculations of the strength of Soviet conventional forces are often deliberately inflated as we shall see in following chapters. A stable balance of military power between East and West demands each side to acknowledge the right of the other to parity in armaments. As Soviet Defence Minister Ustinov put it, 'a rough parity in strategic

nuclear, medium range nuclear weapons, and conventional armaments now exists between the Soviet Union and the United States and between the Warsaw Treaty and NATO'. Both American and Russian leaders affirmed this in the SALT I (Strategic Arms Limitation Talks) treaty, and agreed that this parity was to be maintained. According to the Kremlin it is the Reagan administration which has decided to abandon this previously agreed position and embark on large increases in military spending. If we look back to 1945-65, a time in which the USA possessed undoubted military superiority, we can see that the world was no more peaceful, and indeed perhaps even less peaceful, than it is in the current era of parity. Many Western politicians label the modernisation of existing forces by the USSR as a dangerous threat to peace, and the similar up-grading or modernisation of Western forces as strengthening deterrence.

A sophisticated analysis of Soviet power reveals both its strengths and its weaknesses. An examination of the strengths of the Soviet Army explains both why the West needs its defences, and to some extent what form they should take. An appraisal of its weaknesses shows us both how the system might be defeated and where further effort by the West is not needed.

Even in an age of intercontinental ballistic missiles (ICBMs) and supersonic strike air-

craft an understanding of the influence of geography on Soviet military power is important. The first thing which has to be grasped is the sheer size of the country.

The USSR has a surface area of 22million sq miles and stretches 9,000km from east to west. Its people live in 11 different time zones: as some go to bed in the Ukraine others are on their way to work in the Far East. Its land borders of 20,000km are the longest of any country in the world. The USSR borders on 12 countries: Norway, Finland, Poland, Czechoslovakia, Hungary, Rumania, Turkey, Iran, Afghanistan, China, Mongolia and North Korea. At any one moment Soviet foreign policy must take into account all of these different states with their varying, often contradictory, interests and aspirations. The first military lesson that we must draw from these geographical realities is that in order to defend such a vast country with such long land borders the USSR needs enormous land forces. The second military lesson which we can learn from this geography is that the USSR's forces are spread across the whole breadth of the country and can never be concentrated in their entirety in any one theatre. History shows us that even when the Nazis were only a few miles from the Soviet capital Moscow large forces had to be maintained in the Far East in case the Japanese took advantage of the situation and opened a second front. Soviet fears of a coalition between the NATO countries and Japan or China would force the Russians to do the same in any future war.

The population of the USSR (260million people) is concentrated in European Russia, four-fifths of it living in one-fifth of the land west of the Urals. Within this Soviet heartland is the majority of industry and other economic activity. Of the combined population of the Soviet Union only half are Russians. They are concentrated largely in the Russian Soviet Federated Socialist Republic and are demographically, economically and politically dominant. A Soviet publication notes 'Soviet Russia is rightfully called the first among equals in the single family of fraternal peoples'. Next in

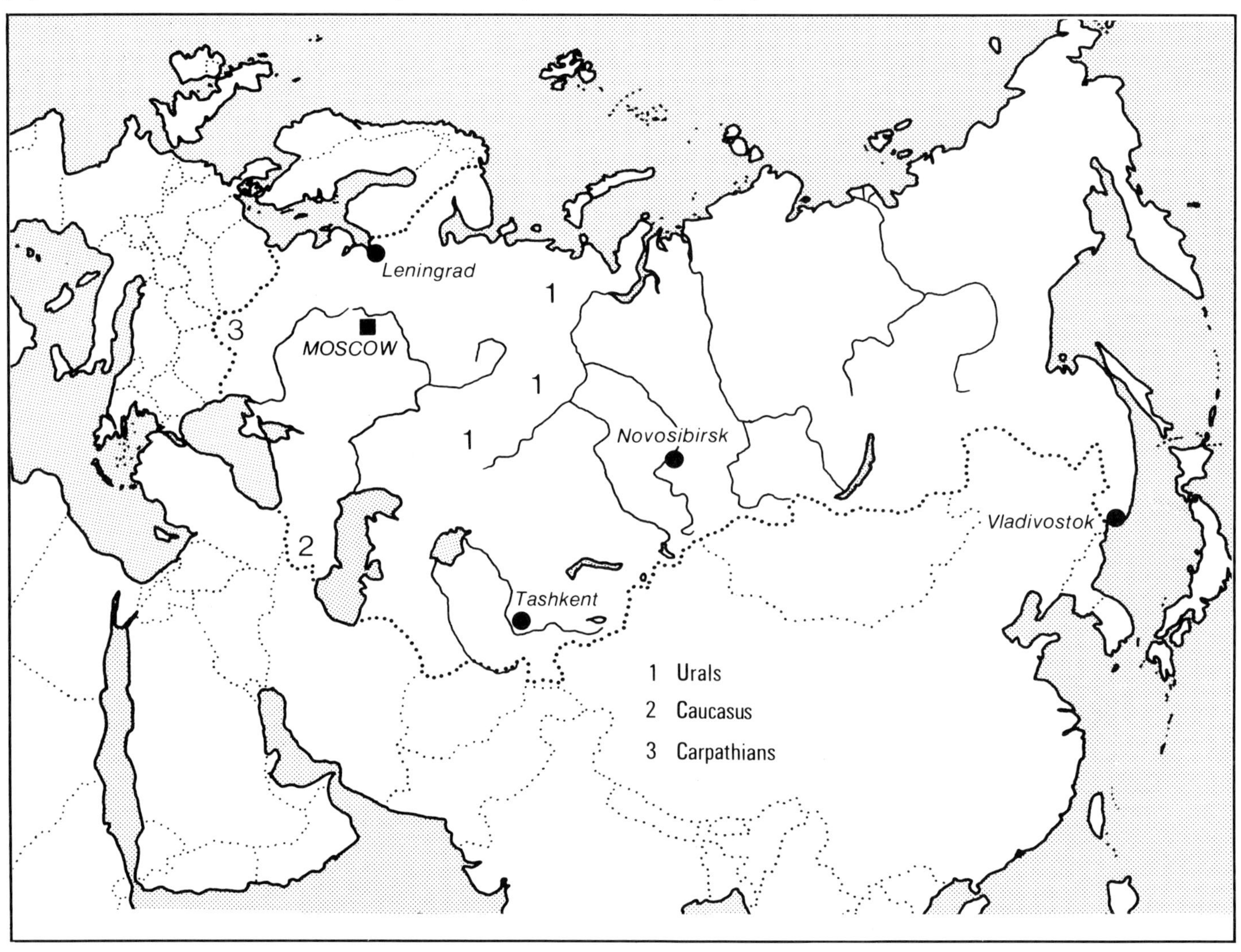

These BTR-70s and BMPs are just part of the enormous amount of hardware produced by Soviet defence industries in the postwar period. *Tass*

importance are the Ukrainians (50million) and Byelorussians (9million), both Slav nationalities with their own culture and heritage. Other important nationalities include those of the Baltic, Caucasian and Central Asian Autonomous Soviet Socialist Republics. The linguistic and physical differences between these people are comparable to that say between a Scotsman and an Algerian: in the USSR there are over 100 officially recognised languages.

Successive rulers of Russia have surrounded the central heartland with a protective barrier. To the west are the east European states allied with the USSR in the Warsaw Pact. In the south are the Caucasus mountains and the empty deserts of Kazakhstan, and to the east the vast Siberian wasteland. The existence of this barrier has a number of strategic consequences. The first is that any aggressor must fight its way across hundreds of miles of eastern Europe, or thousands of miles of emptiness, to reach the heartland and impose a defeat — the armies of both Napoleon and Hitler ran out of steam before they could do this. The other principal strategic consequence is that should the USSR wish to wage war on any one of its neighbours with its land forces it must move men and material from the populated centre to the periphery, an enormous and very hard to disguise logistical undertaking.

The geography of the periphery has resulted in certain areas being better suited to war than others. Historically the invasion armies have marched into Russia via northern Poland and Byelorussia. The central and southern area of Carpathian mountains and Pripet marshes are less well suited to strategic movement. Recent invaders have not tried to breach the Caucasus mountain barrier and the Russians have not fought to secure the area to the south of it. In the east previous conflicts have occurred in Manchuria and the Russian Pacific seaboard rather than in the desert interior (with the exception of the Russo-Japanese border war in Mongolia 1938-39).

The invasion of Russia by Hitler triggered the greatest land conflict in human history. The importance of the Great Patriotic War (as the Soviets call the struggle of 1941-45) to the Soviet Army even today cannot be overestimated.

When the war began the Red Army was unready, even though it had been in the forefront of military developments during the interwar years. The Soviets were, for example, the first to develop the potential of airborne forces. They also realised the importance of armour, and by 1940 had 20,000 tanks in service. Many of these were light models which proved vulnerable to their opponents and they had been scattered throughout the Army in small penny-packets during reorganisations. The reconstruction of large armoured formations was only begun after Zhukov's success with tanks against the Japanese at Khalkin Gol in 1939 and was incomplete when Hitler launched the 'Barbarossa' offensive. More important than the organisational upheaval was the turmoil caused by Stalin's wholesale slaughter of important military cadres. By the outbreak of war three out of five marshals, 60 of the 67 corps commanders and 136 out of 199 divisional commanders had been murdered in the purges.

Stalin's blind faith in the non-aggression pact that he had signed with Hitler in 1939 meant that reports of the German build-up were ignored. And so, perhaps incredibly, when the offensive was launched the Germans had the benefit of complete strategic surprise. So shocked were Stalin and his generals that during the first days of the conflict orders were fragmentary and confused, leading to untold loss of life amongst the forward contingents. Despite many acts of heroism on the part of the Russian soldiery the collapse of command and control, and the superior organisation of the battle-hardened Wehrmacht, brought about one of the most catastrophic defeats in military history. As the Red Army disintegrated under the weight of the blitzkrieg whole armies were encircled and wiped out. Attacks by the Luftwaffe had destroyed most of Russia's front line aircraft on the ground. Between 21 June and 5 December the German forces advanced over 600 miles taking most of European Russia, laying seige to Leningrad and arriving at the gates of Moscow. The initial success of the 'Barbarossa' offensive provided the Soviets both with evidence of how effective suprise is as a weapon and made them determined never to allow another enemy to use it against them.

During the desperate winter of 1941-42 Stalin rallied the Soviet people, and Soviet war industries — many of which had been overrun — were rebuilt in the Urals beyond the range of the Luftwaffe. Whilst this construction was going on the Allies made a vital contribution of tanks, aircraft and materials to the Soviet war effort through the lend-lease programme. Fresh divisions were brought from Siberia and a new Western Front under Zhukov was formed to beat the invaders back from the gates of the capital. In parts of the Ukraine and western Russia the local people had greeted the Axis armies believing themselves to have been freed from the hardships of Stalinism. But the Nazis instituted a regime of mass-murder and barbarism, and whatever goodwill the invaders had first met soon evaporated. Initial partisan activity was limited but brought about such fierce reprisals against the civilian population that the guerillas soon found many new recruits. In time the partisans liberated large areas, disrupted German supply routes and forced them to keep large numbers of troops to protect their rear area.

The battle for Stalingrad on the Volga River is usually regarded as the turning point of the war on the Eastern Front, and indeed by the Soviets as the turning point of the whole war. On the eve of the Soviet counter-offensive of 19 November 1942 the two armies fighting for the city had over a million troops each. The Russians however enjoyed a certain superiorty in artillery and tanks. After heavy fighting the Red Army completed its incirclement of the Axis forces and on 2 February 1943 the battle was concluded with enormous losses of manpower and equipment to the invaders. The steady attrition of the German forces coupled with their defeat at Stalingrad slowly deprived them of the men and weapons needed to initiate major offensive operations. In this way the strategic initiative passed to the Red Army. The German attempts to regain the initiative at Kursk resulted in the greatest armoured battle of the war. Against the advice of many of his generals Hitler ordered the offensive even though repeated delays had forewarned the Russians who prepared extensive fortifications. The failure of this operation doomed the German Army to a defensive role. The tide had turned and the drive to expel the Axis forces had begun.

During the years 1943-45 the Red Army launched successive offensives, with forces that had been restructured to incorporate the lessons of the early part of the war. The new Soviet doctrine embodied and modified some of the principles of the 'lightning war' that had been waged against them. Soviet commanders became obsessed with amassing greater and greater firepower, and the war industries supplied it in greater and greater quantities. Tank armies became the vital instruments of breakthrough, pursuit and encirclement. Artillery was massed in huge amounts with ratios of guns to attack frontage of 100-200 per kilometre being quite normal. It was not of course simply a matter of numbers, for the Supreme Command had brought about dramatic improvements in command and control. The ordinary Russian soldiers proved to be superb fighters, and

(especially after the battles for Moscow and Stalingrad) gained a new fighting spirit. As in most wars the most able commanders came to the fore, and Soviet leadership at the operational (front and army) level was often outstanding. Another hallmark of the Red Army's offensives was the concentration of maximum force in the direction of the main blow. During the Lvov-Sandomir operation for example 80% of the First Ukrainian Front's tanks and 65% of its artillery were concentrated in only 6% of the whole front. These enormous offensives took a great deal of time to plan and supply, and the Red Army often resorted to complex deception plans to disguise its intentions.

The end result of the general offensive of 1943-44 was that the Nazis were expelled from Russia and parts of eastern Europe. In January 1945 Zhukov's First Byelorussian Front and Konev's First Ukranian Front launched the Oder-Vistula operation with the aim of destroying Army Group A and opening the road to Berlin. The initial attacks were conducted on 12 January with a withering artillery barrage in places conducted by 250 guns and mortars per kilometre of attack frontage. By the time the operation ended, Soviet forces had advanced 300 miles and captured key bridges over the Oder (the last obstacle before Berlin), and all in three weeks. On 16 April the Berlin offensive was launched by Zhukov and Konev's fronts. The first phase of the operation, which lasted four days, broke the German defensive line, and the second consisted of encircling and reducing enemy pockets. On 30 April the Red Flag was raised over the Reichstag marking symbolically the victory of the Red Army in Europe, although fighting for Berlin and Prague continued.

The last great offensive of the Great Patriotic War was conducted thousands of miles away in northeast China against Japan's Kwangtung Army. To many analysts the Manchurian offensive represents the highest development of the Soviet war machine of World War 2. Preparation of the operation took place in four well-defined stages. The first was the establishment of a special planning staff drawn from the General Staff, the second the movement of necessary ground forces to the front, followed by the concentration of air assets, and finally the activation of the war command structure. This four-phase pattern has been repeated since the war (for the interventions in Czechoslovakia and Afghanistan), becoming an important part of Soviet military style. Throughout June 1945 the General Staff drew plans for the invasion. Reinforcement of the forces in the Far East with four armies from the western theatre took from May to the end of July. These

Right:
Initially Soviet tanks were deployed in small numbers and were deployed piecemeal. *IWM*

Below right:
The Red Army recovered from its early setbacks and men and machines were forged into an efficient combined-arms fighting force. *Novosti*

forces were moved across Russia on the Trans-Siberian railway — 136,000 wagon loads of men and equipment in all. Three aviation armies were massed by drawing aircraft from the west. On 30 July the planning staff under Marshal Vasilevsky was redesigned as the Headquarters of the Far Eastern Theatre of Military Operations. On 2 August the Transbaikal, 1st Far Eastern and 2nd Far Eastern Fronts were formed and placed along with elements of the Pacific Fleet under Vasilevsky's command. The attack begun on 9 August and consisted of numerous thrusts in the direction of the main cities and airborne landings by diversionary troops. Soviet forces advanced at a phenomenal rate, having launched their attack in a single strategic echelon, with all forces forward. The 6th Guards Tank Army advanced so quickly that it outran its supplies and had to be refuelled by air. Within 12 days most objectives were taken in an area the size of western Europe, although the formal cessation of hostilities only occurred 24 days after the offensive was launched. The hallmarks of the fighting were a daring use of armour and airborne forces leading to terrific advances. There was also a

combined air and seaborne landing to capture the southern half of Sakhalin Island. As writer Ian Hogg put it, 'It was an operation which made Hitler's blitzkrieg look like a horse and cart operation'. What must be remembered is that the Japanese Kwangtung Army was in fact primitive, having something in common with the vanquished Red Army of 1941. Its tanks were light and poorly armed, totally inferior to Soviet T-34s and JSIIs, and they were deployed piecemeal. Large bodies of poorly trained infantry were used without transport, communications or any properly organised system of command and control. The Soviets' whirlwind victory must be viewed with these facts in mind.

As the war ended the Red Army looked upon its achievements. It had played undoubtedly the greatest single part in the defeat of Hitler's Germany. It had also liberated 113million people in Eastern Europe from the evil and darkness of fascist rule.

Soon after the war the ideological conflict known as the Cold War broke out between East and West, breaking the wartime marriage of convenience between the USA, USSR and Britain. In 1949 the Western states formed the North Atlantic Treaty Organisation, an avowedly defensive alliance which nevertheless alarmed the Soviets. Developments in NATO ideology have done something to modify Military Doctrine. Shattered by war and committed to reconstruction the Western states were not prepared to pay for large conventional forces and adopted a policy of nuclear defence. The theory of Massive Retaliation endorsed by NATO throughout the 1950s and early 1960s held that a Soviet advance against the West would be met with a massive nuclear strike. Since those early years of the Alliance the dependence on nuclear weapons has decreased and the size of conventional forces has grown considerably. Whereas in the early 1950s there were only two US Army brigades in Germany there are today two corps, the British Army of the Rhine was of two divisions but is now three, and the West Germans, who had no army when massive

Left:
The general offensive in eastern Europe culminated in the Berlin operation. *Tass*

Below left:
The raising of the Red Flag over the Reichstag marked symbolically the defeat of Nazi Germany. *Novosti*

Below:
Steamroller in action: a mechanised column pauses during the August 1945 Manchurian operation. An area the size of western Europe was seized in two weeks. *Novosti*

Bottom:
During the 1960s much energy was devoted to training for war in nuclear conditions. *via C. F. Foss*

The General Offensive, January 1944–May 1945.

Operation	Av rates of advance (km/day)	Max rates of advance (km/day)	Superiority in tanks	Superiority in artillery
Iassi-Kishinev	40-50	70	6:1	8:1
Lvov-Sandomir	20	50	10:1	7:1
Oder-Vistula	30	75-90	10:1	7:1
Berlin	20	50	6:1	6:1
Manchuria	100	160	5:1	5:1

retaliation was adopted today contribute three corps to the NATO order of battle. These increases in conventional forces followed agreement by the allies that the massive retaliation doctrine was losing credibility. A new strategy called Flexible Response was evolved which would meet Soviet thrusts with conventional or nuclear weapons depending on which was necessary.

The Great Patriotic War and developments within NATO not only affected broad Soviet policy — Military Doctrine — but also Military Art, which is the theory and practice of engaging in operations and armed conflict as a whole. Military Art defines three inter-related levels of warfare: Strategic (national war strategy, theatre commands), Operational (at the front and army level), and Tactical (division and below). Military Art also recognises a number of principles of war and these were enumerated by Col V. Savkin in the important work *Basic Principles of Operational Art and Tactics*.

1: Mobility and High Tempos of Combat Operations

The adoption of flexible response by NATO resulted in an even greater emphasis on speed of advance. If an offensive could seize enough territory quickly enough then NATO could be defeated before the decision could be taken for nuclear release. Only a highly mobile army can take advantage of nuclear strikes before the enemy has had a chance to

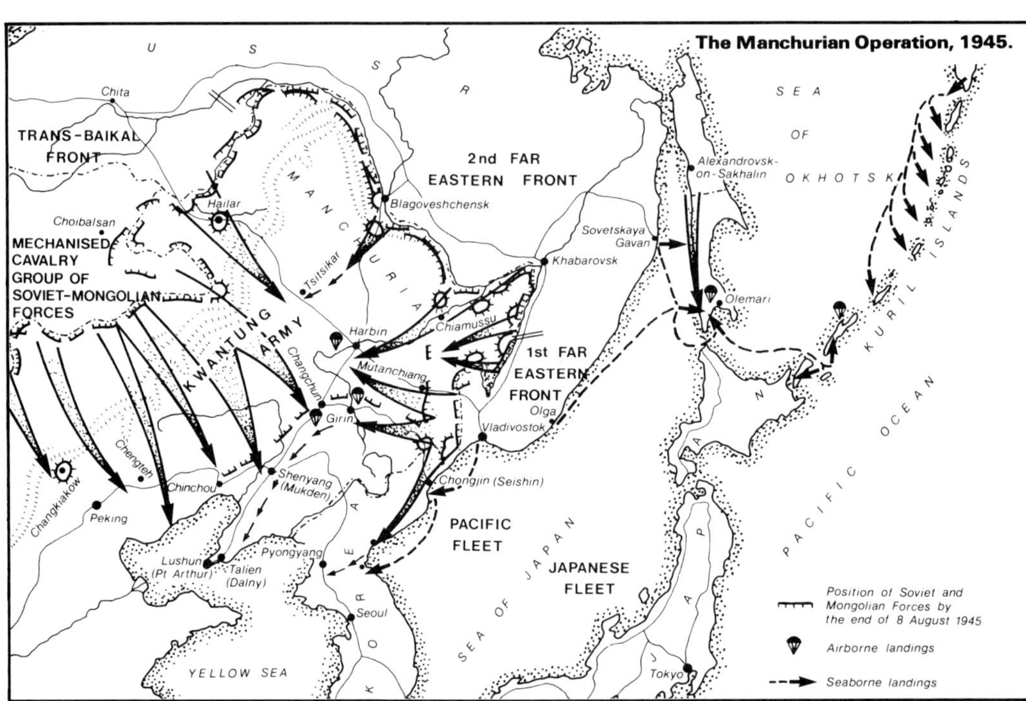

regroup. The most mobile elements, the air-landed troops, are the best suited to the 'timely exploitation of nuclear strikes'.

Savkin's concept of mobility extends beyond the actual mechanisation of forces. It embraces 'the capability for the rapid and most effective accomplishment of the combat mission and for manoeuvre and reaction to any change in the situation, even the most abrupt one; high tempo activity; their ease of control; flexibility in using firepower; the capability of quickly identifying targets for delivering strikes against the enemy; flexibility of thinking of the commanders; precision in organising control and materiel and technical support; and the ability to operate at the necessary moment and at the necessary place faster than the enemy and unexpectedly for him' (Savkin).

The ability of modern mechanised forces to cross rivers gives them an advantage over the armoured forces of World War 2. Army-

Gen Kurochkin stated that 'modern tank forces have incomparably greater possibilities of crossing rivers both with the aid of various mechanised river crossing equipment and by themselves under water'.

The emphasis on high tempos and offensive action in Soviet tactics should not be taken as evidence of an aggressive overall policy. As P. H. Vigor put it 'The tactics are offensive because... they offer to the Marxist military mind the sole hope of victory in a war with the West. Tactics based on the defensive would, the Russians believe, be certain to lose such a war'.

2: Concentration of Efforts

As our all too brief examination of the Great Patriotic War showed concentration of efforts in the direction of the main blow was an important part of past Soviet offensives. There is however an inherent conflict caused by the need to concentrate so as to achieve decisive results and the risk of doing this in an environment where nuclear weapons might be used. The Soviets recognise the problem: 'under conditions of the constant threat of enemy use of nuclear weapons the concentration of disposition of a large number of troops in limited regions is highly unsafe' (Maj-Gen S. Shtrik in *Military Thought*, January 1968). Concentrations of the kind achieved on the Eastern Front might well prove impossible in future. NATO con-

ventional artillery and airpower would prevent the concentrations of artillery of the type achieved in the Oder-Vistula operation. The pressure of time would be so accute that most attacks would have to be launched 'from the march' without the benefits of planning and logistical build-up that preceded breakthrough operations against the Wehrmacht.

The development of Western non-nuclear systems such as the Assault Breaker which can stop armoured thrusts with conventional sub-munitions is also very important in the connection. The Soviet Army has hoped to minimise the risks of concentration by insisting that it be done with such speed that an enemy simply wouldn't have time to target and launch a nuclear attack. However the introduction of the US Pave Mover radar and its associated systems will give NATO commanders a 'real time' picture of Soviet concentrations and allow them to react quickly enough to neutralise them with conventional or nuclear weapons. The concentration factor is therefore a problematical one, but it is important to understand that the Soviet Army will concentrate, despite the risks, to achieve the breakthroughs it needs in offensive operations.

3: Surprise

At all levels of Military Art surprise is considered to be a most important ingredient in victory. Where there is approximate equality of forces it is seen as the means of gaining a decisive advantage. Deft use of surprise actions will cause panic and disorder among enemy forces and may lead to a collapse of his command system.

In the Great Patriotic War though the Red Army was as vulnerable to surprise as any other, perhaps more so because of the lack of initiative accorded to junior commanders. The use of deception will play an important part in Soviet attempts to launch surprise attacks. During the Great Patriotic War considerable engineering resources were devoted to faking concentration areas, bridges, roads and vehicles so as to wrong-foot the enemy as to the real direction of an impending attack.

4: Combat Activeness

Soviet writers devote a great deal of attention to the idea of seizing and retaining the initiative. Soviet officers are exhorted to adopt a highly aggressive style of command and to put the enemy under constant pressure and exploit his mistakes wherever possible. Combat activeness is just as important in defence — the aim being to weaken the enemy sufficiently for there to be a resumption of the offensive.

The successful practice of the kind of bold advance that Soviet doctrine deems necessary requires a highly capable officer corps and a well-developed system of troop control. Savkin emphasises the high professional standards and elan required of the Soviet officer: 'Active operations here are characterised by extreme decisiveness and swiftness of reaction to a constantly changing situation. A lack of information about the enemy cannot serve as the reason for rejection of bold actions'. An important part of seizing the initiative is the anticipation and pre-emption of enemy actions. This factor has important implications in the first use of nuclear weapons. A Soviet guarantee of no first use is meaningless without a similar undertaking by NATO, for Military Doctrine makes it clear that an enemy cannot be allowed to enjoy the benefits which a first use of nuclear weapons might confer.

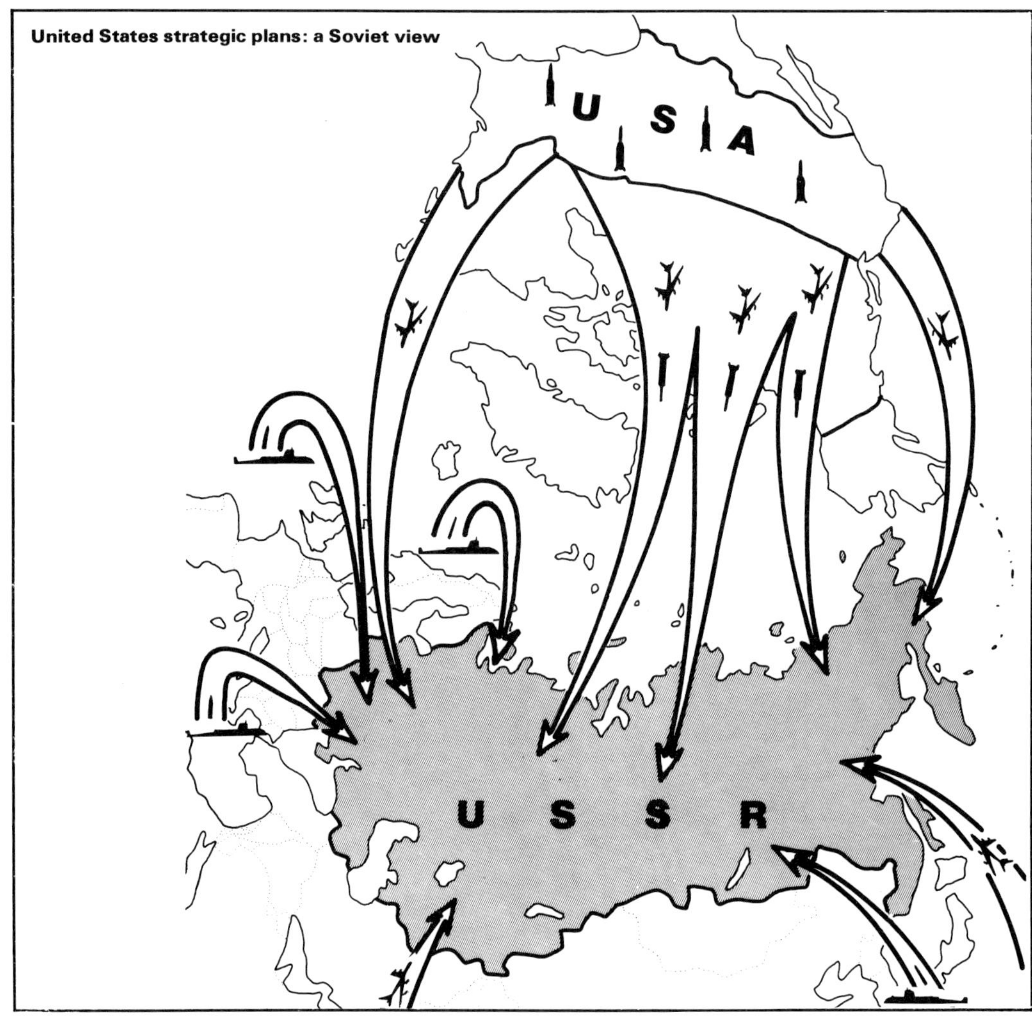

5: Preservation of Combat Effectiveness of Friendly Troops

In order that formations might be able to fulfil their missions it is essential that they remain sufficiently strong. This is especially important in nuclear conditions where a single nuclear burst could traumatise or disable an entire division. Soviet writers have suggested a number of ways in which combat effectiveness might be maintained.

One of the most important in both conventional and nuclear operations is the echelonment of forces. Echelons are specifically tasked forces developed in depth in the Army. They became very popular with commanders during the war when they provided a means of breaching successive German positional defences; a front for example tasked one or more armies to exploit the success of the first echelon. Second echelon armies could also be used to replace forces which had lost their combat effectiveness. Badly depleted units could also be combined with others to re-form effective formations.

Soviet theorists also stress the importance

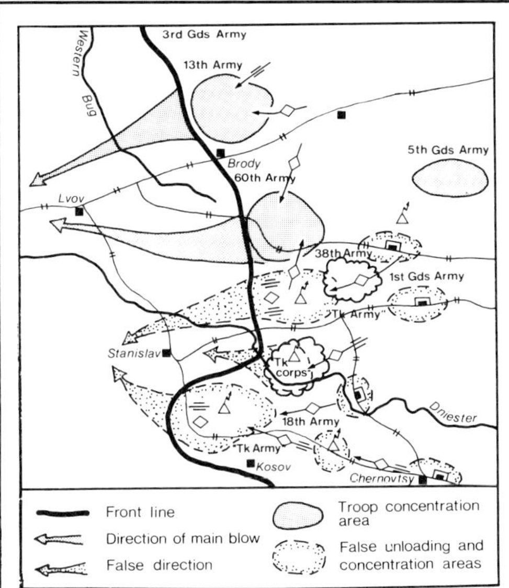

Operational Deception during the Lvov–Sandomir operation

Soviet textbooks cite this deception operation as a model one. In order to disguise their push towards Lvov and key bridges over the Vistula, measures were taken to convince the Germans that a major attack would be launched farther south, in the Stanislav direction. Engineers built 1,000 dummy tanks and 1,300 mock gun emplacements in order to convince the enemy that a new army was being massed. Tank engine noises were broadcast by loudspeakers and troops in the area intentionally observed poor discipline, making themselves visible to enemy reconnaissance. In tandem with these measures strict security was enforced farther north, where the real breakthrough was about to be launched. The result: the Germans moved two divisions to reinforce Stanislav and the Red Army broke through their lines and advanced towards Lvov rapidly.

of maintaining personal combat-effectiveness. Great store is set by morale-boosting political work to keep the troops' spirits up, especially when nuclear or chemical weapons have been used. Like their NATO counterparts Soviet officers would have difficulty delivering rousing patriotic speeches with their gasmasks on.

6: Confirmity of the Goal of the Operation to Conditions of the Actual Situation

The goal of any operation must be formulated only after a careful appraisal of the forces available to each side and the factors likely to favour one or the other. A careful formulation of the goal by field-force commanders is important if their subordinates are to be able to carry out the missions assigned to them. Soviet manuals warn against both underestimating and over-estimating the enemy as this might result in defeat or the loss of the initiative. There is something of a conflict between the need to estimate opponents' strengths carefully and Savkin's earlier point that a lack of information about the enemy is no excuse to avoid bold action.

7: Interaction

This last principle emphasises combined-arms co-operation at all levels. As Col Skovorodkin of the General Staff Academy wrote, 'Soviet Military Doctrine considers that victory in a modern war can be achieved only by the combined efforts of the armed forces. . . . The stated principle applies not only to war in its entirely but also to major strategic operations and even more so to operations carried out by individual branches of the armed forces'. Recent command changes in the armed forces emphasise the close inter-relationship of all arms at the strategic and operational levels.

These principles of war govern the execution of missions and constitute the essence of the Soviet style in war. Operations are divided into four types: the offensive, the break-through, pursuit and defence. We shall simplify things somewhat by examining offence and defence.

The Offensive

'The offensive is the basic form of combat action. Only by a resolute offensive conducted at a high tempo and to great depth is the total destruction of the enemy maintained' (Gen V. Reznichenko). The

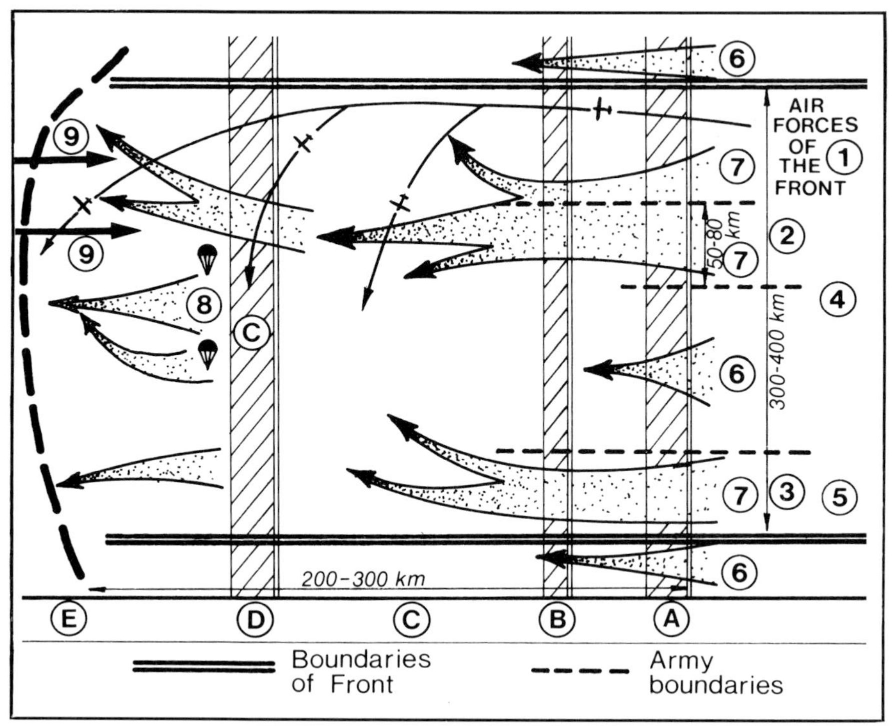

A stylised offensive operation by a front during World War 2

1 — Air assault corps; *2* — Front tank forces; *3* — Front tank forces; *4* — Reserve army; *5* — Reserve rifle corps; *6* — Rifle army; *7* — Breakthrough army; *8* — Drop zone; *9* — Enemy reinforcements.

A — Attack launched on first line of defence. Breakthrough armies attack on narrow frontages with powerful tank forces in reserve. Neighbouring fronts co-ordinate simultaneous strikes.
B — Enemy second line breached. Second echelon tank forces committed.
C — Tank forces spread out to exploit breakthrough. Air assault forces land to engage enemy reinforcements.
D — Last line of defence breached. Link-up with air-landed forces.
E — Final objective.

Soviet Army believes that final victory in war can only be won by offensive action.

Prior to the launching of a general offensive there will be fire preparation by aviation, artillery and missiles. Whether the Soviets would make an initial nuclear strike prior to an offensive against western Europe is a moot point. For many years it has certainly been the assumption of many Soviet strategists that they would. Col Samoukov wrote in *Military Thought*, 'Combat operations without the use of nuclear weapons independent of the development of events cannot be of long duration'. The benefits that could be gained by an early nuclear strike seem irresistible to many Soviet theoreticians: 'pre-emption in launching a nuclear strike is considered to be the decisive condition for the attainment of superiority over him and the seizure and retention of the initiative' (Col A. A. Sikorenko in *The Offensive*). However, balanced against this enthusiasm must be the near certainty of retaliation and the fact that even a theatre level nuclear exchange would flatten much of the territory that the protagonists were fighting for.

In an offensive field-forces will be assigned axes and areas of responsibility. A front will advance through an area 200-230km across, and an army one 40-80km across. Objectives are divided into immediate, long range and strategic. Immediate objectives may involve advances of 250km over three-five days and are the responsibility of divisions and armies. Long range objectives extend into an enemy's operational depth up to 560km and would be attained in 12-14 days under the responsibility of armies and fronts. Final objectives 1,000km or more in depth may be attained after three weeks and are the responsibility of the theatre command. Planning and combat actions at divisional level will concentrate solely on immediate tactical objectives and so on.

During the initial phase of an offensive both sides will attempt to gain the initiative and most battles will take the form of meeting engagements. The meeting engagement places particular demands on the commander who must prepare his battle plans and launch attacks from the march. Under these circumstances Soviet doctrine holds that victory will go to the more aggressive and determined commander as there will be little time to concentrate firepower and support elements. Meeting engagements will often be fought by advanced guard battalions at the head of regimental columns. These battalions will be reinforced with artillery and engineer elements. So as to maintain momentum guard battalions may attempt to bypass important enemy strong-points. According to the Russians the increased mechanisation of forces and introduction of air-landed troops make meeting engagements both more likely and more important. Particular importance is attached to the order of march within regimental columns as this will determine how quickly the commander can introduce various elements into the battle. Because these flying columns must move at such high speed they are only able to carry limited amounts of ammunition.

By use of delaying tactics and prepared positions an enemy may take the momentum out of an attacking force. In these circumstances it is imperative that commanders take every step to break the enemy defence .and resume the fastest possible advance. 'Deliberate' or breakthrough attacks must then be launched to dislodge the foe. A great deal more time can be spent on these than on attacks from the march, allowing units to mass their armour and bring up sufficient ammunition for a withering artillery barrage. There are of course risks in doing this and the breakthrough force would be given more problems by a NATO-style mobile or active defence.

Tactical as well as strategic nuclear weapons were introduced in the 1960s. These 'Scud-A' systems were fielded to give army-level commanders their own nuclear firepower. *Novosti*

A Warsaw Pact response to the soundness of current NATO defence plans has been the increased importance of the Operational Manoeuvre Groups (OMG). These groups consist of strengthened divisions or larger forces and would break the front line penetrating deep into the NATO rear. They would attack nuclear weapon sites, supply echelons, airfields and lines of defence in depth and thus hope to bring about the collapse from within of NATO forces. Once these forces were committed in the rear the enemy would be unable to use nuclear weapons against them for fear of damaging friendly forces and the local civilian population. Although some Western analysts claim that the popularity of the OMG concept among Warsaw Pact strategists is a recent thing, it has in fact been discussed by them in detail since the mid-1960s. Army-Gen Kurochkin described the use of OMGs in the war in 1967 in *Military Thought*: 'These mobile groups developed the attack and carried on the pursuit, as a rule on separate axes, independent of the main forces of the fronts and armies, forced water barriers from the march, and with preparation in limited periods'. He added 'now also separate tank groups can be established and function independently during operations, to a great extent separate from the main attacking forces'. NATO's best hope of stopping OMGs lies in the use of attack helicopters, remotely laid minefields and liberal use of anti-tank missiles. The use of OMGs is not without risk for should the defender rally and shore up the breach in his front line the mobile group will find itself deep in enemy territory with limited supplies and combat resources.

Whatever form of attack the Soviets use, one of their main aims will be to break the enemy and begin a pursuit. 'Pursuit represents an attack on a withdrawing enemy for the purpose of final destruction (or capture) of his forces' (Col Sidorenko in *The Offensive*). They would aim during the pursuit to remain in contact with their foe and thus prevent him from regrouping to form an effective defence. During a pursuit the greatest gains may be made, and logistics norms stipulate higher fuel consumption than for any other type of combat action.

Vitally important to the Soviet Army's ability to keep moving forward at break-neck speed is the ability to breach water barriers by assault river crossings. These are divided into hasty crossings which are unopposed or weakly opposed, and deliberate crossings

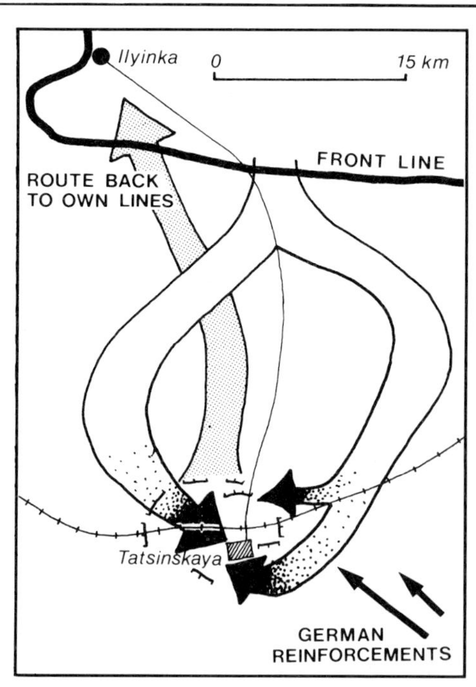

OMGs — an example from the Great Patriotic War

An operational group based on the 24th Tank Corps spent 13 days behind German lines in December 1942. During the raid on Tatsinskaya station and its nearby airfield it spread havoc, killing over 11,000 enemy troops and destroying over 400 aircraft. Several German divisions had to be diverted from other sectors in order to repel the breakthrough. The raiding group returned to Red Army lines where it was redesignated the 2nd Guards Tatsin Tank Corps.

against a well-prepared defence. Large amounts of specialised equipment have been developed by the Warsaw Pact to allow these operations to be conducted so quickly that there is no overall loss of momentum by the advancing forces. Deliberate crossings present more problems and careful planning is required to make a success of them. They would normally be carried out at night and with considerable support. The success of the Egyptians in their assault crossing of the Suez Canal in 1973 shows the soundness of Soviet doctrine and equipment in this field.

The Defence

The Soviets believe that during the offensive they may at times be forced to assume the defensive until the enemy can be sufficiently weakened for a a resumption of the attack. In some theatres (particularly in the Far East) they might be surprised by superior forces and forced to assume a strategic defence for some time. Defensive frontages will vary widely — a division for example might hold anything from 10 to 40km. Defensive forces are divided into a number of elements. In the prepared defence a security echelon of light forces will act as a delaying and covering screen. Behind them will be the main defence

belt, and then the reserve. Tank forces will usually be assigned to the latter ready to deliver a counter-blow should an enemy attack break through or falter.

During the Great Patriotic War, at Kursk for example, successive belts of entrenched infantry and anti-tank guns were laboriously prepared. Under modern nuclear conditions there would probably not be the time to construct such fortifications. Rapidly advancing forward elements may run into strong enemy forces and find themselves assuming a hasty defence. Attempts may be made to break contact and occupy better positions, and a tank element may be detached to act as a covering force. The offensive will be resumed as soon as strong enough forces have been brought forward. The Yom Kippur War showed how effective the Russian-style defence using anti-tank weapons can be in the right circumstances.

Permission to withdraw from an untenable position can only be given by a superior commander. Withdrawals will wherever possible be carried out at night, and on as many routes as possible so as to prevent concentration. A covering force will be left in contact with the enemy and a rearguard deployed to hinder attempts at pursuit.

Combat Support

The mass barrages of guns placed wheel to wheel that took place in the war are no longer possible under modern conditions. Postwar years have seen the decentralisation of artillery assets to regiments and divisions. This has resulted in the commanders at the front having instant and flexible dedicated fire support. Recently several models of self-propelled gun have been introduced to give the guns the same mobility that is enjoyed by the other arms.

In war Soviet artillery divisions and brigades might gain or lose individual battalions on a temporary basis, being very much tailored to meet specific missions. Thus a division might be assigned a battalion of M-1946 130mm guns for counter-battery missions from army resources. In many respects the tactics and operations of artillery have changed more than those of the other arms. Many guns are now nuclear capable, and the risks of counter-battery fire and high tempo of operations has forced many changes in the command and control of the guns.

The soundness of Soviet ideas on air defence support has been proven in a number of local wars. An integrated web of over-

The Assault River Crossing

Top left:
H–3. Reconnaissance elements reach the river and make their way across under enemy fire to locate suitable landing points. *via C. F. Foss*

Above left:
H–Hour. Preceded by a heavy artillery barrage lasting half an hour the first motor rifle battalion crosses in its BMPs. Smoke is laid to conceal their progress and the guns switch to targets in depth as they reach the bank. *Novosti*

Top:
H+1. The first tank rolls across the divisional pontoon bridge. *ADN*

Above:
H+2. Divisional combat elements have crossed the bridge and support units begin to join them. *ADN*

lapping systems is designed to make life as difficult as possible for enemy aviation. Since 1981 anti-aircraft forces in army units have fallen under the control of the Air Defence Forces (PVO). This enables a single command authority at army, front or theatre level to make decisions concerning the engagement of hostile aircraft. This new command system which integrates interceptors, radar stations and anti-aircraft units may also make the business of IFF (Identification Friend or Foe) more straightforward. An important lesson of the 1973 Middle East war which should not be overlooked is that the whole advance of Egyptian forces which had crossed the Suez Canal had to be held up whilst air defence units were moved forward.

Recent organisational changes in Frontal Aviation have altered the nature of tactical air support. Frontal Aviation forces have been streamlined and reorganised at the theatre level (which is not to say that aviation regiments might not still be assigned to armies or fronts). Ground Forces divisions are now being assigned helicopter elements for support. This marks something of a departure from previous practice and is analogous to the decentralisation of artillery assets. Whilst providing more flexible on-call tactical support it also makes the concentration of force more difficult.

Soviet armies and fronts are equipped with organic Radio Electronic Combat (REC, or Electronic Warfare) resources. Capabilities are organised into direction-finding, interception and jamming. Missions will include communications and intelligence reconnaissance, electronic countermeasures and electronic support measures.

The successful practice of combat or support operations, and the practice of Military Doctrine and Military Art, require efficiency of command, communications and control. The Soviets distinguish between national/strategic command, which they call the Direction of the Armed Forces, and operational/tactical command, which they call Troop Control; together they are the nervous system of the Soviet Army.

2. ORGANISING THE JUGGERNAUT

★

COMMAND, CONTROL AND INTELLIGENCE

The structure of both political and military authority in the USSR is indeed complex. Constitutionally the Supreme Soviet is the principal organ of government, having two chambers with a combined total of around 1,500 members. At election time the population sends representatives (chosen by the Party, and often holding other important posts) to the Supreme Soviet. Although it has important legal and symbolic roles (including the right to declare war) it is not the centre of real political power in the USSR. This lies with the Central Committee of the CPSU, and its elected caucus in Politburo. Because the 320-odd members of the Central Committee all hold prestigious appointments in the Party, the economy, the arts and sciences, and the armed forces, the full Central Committee only meets twice a year, although extraordinary meetings can be called. Day to day it is the working groups of the Central Committee, and in particular the Politburo, which make policy. The Politburo usually stands at around a dozen members, is chaired by the CPSU General Secretary (currently Konstantin Chernenko) and includes the Minister of Defence (Marshal D. F. Ustinov), the Minister of the Interior and other key Party officials. The CPSU Central Committee Secretariat is another powerful organ responsible for administering the working groups, and the Party machine in general. The third arm of power in the Soviet Union is the Council of Ministers which co-ordinates the execution of policies.

The organs for the Direction of the Armed Forces are structured differently in peace and war. In peacetime broad decisions of national policy such as 'shall we give fraternal assistance to Czechoslovakia?' are decided by the Politburo. Wherever possible it seeks the endorsement of the Central Committee. More detailed measures are then hammered out in the Council of Defence. Membership of the Council of Defence, which is chaired by Konstantin Chernenko, consists of key politburo members with security-related briefs (eg Defence Minister and Foreign Minister) and perhaps two or three key military men. In addition to the half-dozen regular members there are a number of places taken by experts in particular fields who are co-opted on to the Council for particular discussions. In 1970 for example the Council of Defence sat to consider Egyptian requests for defence against Israeli air strikes. Egyptian sources tell us that around 20 people sat on the Council, half of whom were military men including a number of experts from the Air Defence Forces. The Council agreed to send a number of air defence batteries and several thousand advisors.

Much of what goes on in the Council of Defence is probably determined by the Main Military Council of the Ministry of Defence, the two organisations having members in common. It is chaired by the minister and includes four first deputy ministers (the Chief of the General Staff, C-in-C of the Warsaw Pact, Chief of the Main Political Administration, and one first deputy for 'general affairs' (who seems to act as the minister's trouble shooter) and 10 deputy ministers. These are the heads of the five armed services (Strategic Rocket, Ground, Air Defence, Air and Naval forces) plus the chiefs of Rear Services, Construction, Civil Defence, Defence Industry

and the Inspector General. Their principal business consists of sorting out day-to-day matters of training, administration and liaison. It is also in this body that the armed forces draw up their own planning and resource requirements and determine exactly which service gets what slice of the defence cake.

Each of the service chiefs who sits on the Main Military Council reports back to his own Military Council. They in turn work out the administrative arrangements for their individual branches of service. Whilst the Ground Forces branch headquarters such as Tank Troops have important peacetime work in organising training they would have no real part to play in the wartime operational command of these forces. It is important to note the importance of military councils in the Soviet command system. These are chaired by the commander of the formation, or head of service — in short, whoever is in charge. They work in the principle of democratic centralism by which members are bound by collective decisions even if they themselves have argued against them. In this

way it is hoped that consensus between a commander and his subordinates will be maintained. To be sure, it is not a 'free for all' because the chairman will outrank the other members of the collective and is in a position to manipulate the course of the discussion. Also of interest is the role of first deputies in the Soviet military. They are usually experienced men who are being schooled to succeed as commander, although this is not inevitable. So, the first deputy commander of a Military District will usually take over as commander of one. Interestingly the overall command of Soviet interventions in recent years has always been taken by a first deputy: in Czechoslovakia and Ethiopia by the First Deputy Commander of Ground Forces, and in the case of Afghanistan by the First Deputy Minister of Defence. Clearly as the men destined for promotion they were considered both the most capable and the most in need of high level command experience.

In war membership of the national command organisations would change in a number of ways. The Council of Defence of military and political leaders would become the State Committee for Defence charged with directing the entire national war effort. There would be little time to refer back to the Central Committee, or indeed the full Politburo, so its proclamations would automatically have the force of law. The Main Military Council of the Ministry of Defence would be transformed into the Supreme High Command, known in the Great Patriotic War by its Russian initials VGK. The General Sec-

retary would chair this in his role as 'Supreme C-in-C' of Soviet forces. It is likely that the commander-in-chief of theatres of military operations would displace a number of the lesser service chiefs in importance on the Command. Within the Supreme High Command key issues concerning the course of the war and the relative importance of the theatres would be worked out. The transformation of the Main Military Council into the Supreme High Command would take place shortly before the outbreak of hostilities.

In both war and peace the responsibility for the implementation of the decisions of the military leadership lies with the General Staff. In the Soviet Union the General Staff has a critical role both in the preparation of the agendas of the highest military councils, and in the translation of its deliberations into practical directives to the force commanders. According to Western analysts Marshal Akhromeyev the Chief of the General Staff, ranks third only to the minister in the defence hierarchy. The General Staff includes officers from all of the services but is dominated by men of the Soviet Army. It combines the functions of think-tank, intelligence network and executive arm of the military leadership. The Staff is organised into a number of directorates including the Operations, Intelligence, Organisation and Mobilisation, and Foreign Military Assistance Main Directorates. Other departments are responsible for communications, cartography, developing new weapons and planning strategic movement. Sections of the Operations Main Directorate are responsible

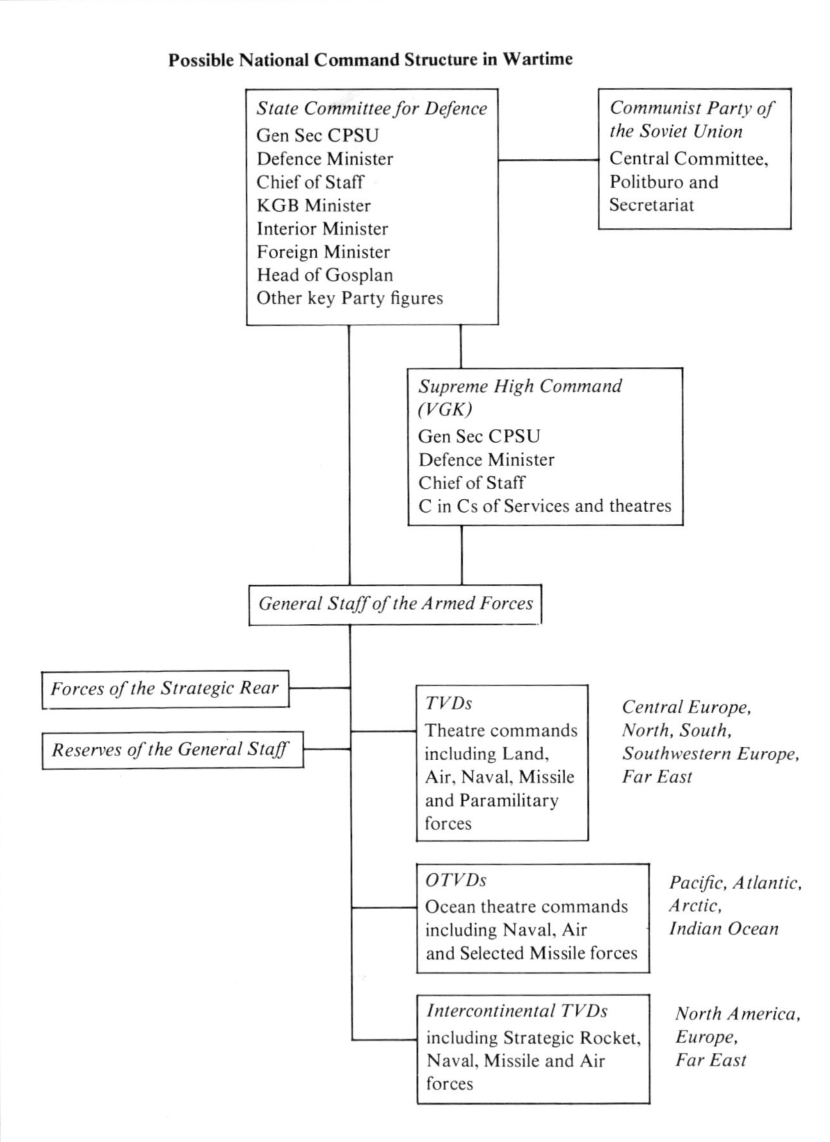

1 — Politburo and Central Committee remain highly important, but would often be set aside to speed up crisis decision making.

2 — Detailed military policy would be hammered out in the VGK.

3 — Some critical decisions of the State Committee for Defence would be executed immediately by the General Staff, by-passing the VGK.

4 — Reserves would include air assault divisions, selected ground forces and several missile divisions of the Strategic Rocket Forces.

5 — Forces of the Strategic Rear would include reserve divisions being brought up to strength, and logistic railway, construction, paramilitary and civil defence forces.

for contingency planning in various theatres. The Staff plays a critical role in detabes on force structure and military doctrine. The Voroshilov Academy is also part of the organisation and plays an important role in instructing Warsaw Pact officers in new ideas. Finally the Staff plays the leading part in formulating the USSR's detailed position in international arms talks. *The Times* has described Col-Gen Nikolai Cherkov (of the Staff) as 'the arms control mouthpiece of the new (Andropov) regime'.

Another influential organ of the Ministry of Defence is the Main Political Administration (MPA), which also has the status of a Central Committee department. Perhaps for political reasons some Western observers are sceptical about its usefulness. Some have tried to paint a picture of organisational conflict between military commanders and their political deputies, and indeed between Army and Party in general. Because the Soviet system is one of consensus within the CPSU it follows that the military can not always have its own way, and occasionally this causes resentment. But the vast majority of Army officers are Party members and those who reach high ranks will have worked on Party organisations throughout their careers. It is unlikely that their view of the world and of CPSU policy differs in any major way from that of the Party bosses. Marshal Ogarkov represented the rare example of a Soviet military man who put his views forward in public. In May 1984 he published an article saying that the acquisition of more nuclear weapons was 'senseless'. This outspokenness (by Soviet standards) lost him his job in September of the same year.

The Chief of the MPA, Gen A. A. Yepishev, is one of the most respected figures in the military hierarchy. His role as a Party supremo in uniform places him in a unique position of trust. Personal visits by Yepishev to Czechoslovakia in 1968 and Afghanistan in 1979 before the interventions in those two countries point to an important tole as the CPSU's man in uniform. He also acts as an arbitrator between branches of the services, settling problems over the allocation of resources, among other things.

Under Yepishev are an estimated 100,000 political workers in uniform throughout the Army and Fleet. Political deputies sit on military councils from theatre to unit level. At the high level they will also usually sit on local government committees trying to assure smooth relations between civil and military authorities. At the low level they are involved in the practical work of being an officer in battalion headquarters as well as running primary Party organisations. The MPA also plays an important role in lecturing the troops on current affairs and informing them of Party policy. It is impossible to quantify the real influence of the MPA, but doubtless

it serves to reassure politicians that the Army is not developing what the Soviets would call 'bonapartist' (ie political) ambitions, and provides the Army with another method of communicating with the politicians. Certainly an MPA Chief is able to carve for himself a position of considerable influence. An important role that Yepishev and his organisation have played is in the cementing of Warsaw pact unity.

Practically speaking it is impossible to look at Soviet land power without examining the command structure of the Warsaw Pact. The Pact, or Warsaw Treaty Organisation (WTO) as it is properly known, plays a number of important roles. According to the Soviets it is purely defensive and has since its formation in May 1955 safeguarded eastern Europe from attack by NATO. Certainly the WTO has an important role in integrating east European defence but what form that defence takes (attack being the best form of defence in many people's eyes) is another question.

The Pact has a number of organs, many of which, like the Supreme Soviet, serve a symbolic role. The Political Consultative Committee consists of national leaders meeting once or twice a year to co-ordinate foreign/military policies. Similarly the Committee of Defence Ministers meets occasionally to mull over high level issues. The Committee of Foreign Ministers and Military Council allow interactions at the foreign minister and deputy defence minister levels respectively. All of the political and military/political bodies are used to show Soviet bloc unity on security issues. The practical military work of the WTO is carried out by the Joint Command and Staff. Col-Gen Sredin, First Deputy Chief of the MPA, states that it 'co-ordinates efforts in the field of military con-

struction and training of the Joint Armed Forces, equipment of the allied armies with materiel, improvement of the organisation of the forces and raising their military potentials'. Sredin and other Soviet generals do not pretend that the Pact has a major role to play in the war command of Eastern bloc field formations. In this respect the WTO differs quite markedly from NATO with its unified combat headquarters.

The WTO's principal role is in the co-ordination of training by the armed forces of its members. Large scale exercises such as 'Brotherhood in Arms 80' are examples of WTO planning. Within the Eastern bloc there are also many bilateral contacts between the USSR and other members. These are just as important as it is often during these meetings between east European and Soviet generals that new policies and doctrines are discussed frankly. These bilateral contacts, unlike WTO meetings, are not surrounded by publicity and do not have to end in a show of unanimity.

The Soviet and Non-Soviet Warsaw Pact (NSWP) armed forces which take part in combined manoeuvres are referred to as the Joint Armed Forces. The Soviet contribution consists of its Groups of Forces in eastern Europe and certain formations in its western MDs. NSWP states have assigned roughly half of their national forces to the Joint Armed Forces, representing their highest readiness and most mechanised formations. East German divisions have in the past conducted operations under the direct command of Soviet army HQs. Most integration would probably however take place at frontal level, with entire armies coming under Soviet command.

The Joint Armed Forces are divided into northern and southern tiers. The northern

forces are those of East Germany, Poland and Czechoslovakia and the southern tier of Hungary, Rumania and Bulgaria. It is generally agreed that the southern tier forces are lower on the list of equipment and modernisation priorities. The military doctrines of these states (with the exception of Rumania) is patterned after the Soviet model. Many east European officers are trained in Soviet academies, and all but one of the NSWP defence ministers are graduates of the Voroshilov General Staff Academy in Moscow. Although east European generals have taken charge of large WTO exercises (for example, 'Shield 79' manoeuvres were supervised by a Hungarian general), there is no real evidence to suppose that they would be given command of Soviet forces above divisional level in war. The Soviets hold all of the key WTO positions: C-in-C, Chief of Staff (and First Deputy C-in-C) and Chief of Air Defence Forces.

There are two fields in which Pact commands would have a role to play in war. These are the Air Defence and Combined Baltic Commands. In each a Soviet officer commands what is in essence a theatre-level war organisation. NSWP Air Defence and Baltic naval forces (as well as certain logistics and communications units) are already under joint (ie Soviet) rather than national command.

One question which is often asked in the West is how reliable NSWP states would be in a war with the West? Certainly some would be readier to participate than others — the East Germans and Bulgarians being the 'keenest'. The Polish Army is the largest of the NSWP states and seemed to have no moral qualms about taking part in the Czechoslovak intervention, or indeed the imposition of martial law in its own country. Indeed the only country that would definitely not deploy its forces abroad as its constitution forbids it is Rumania. The military elites of eastern Europe are schooled by the Russians, and many senior generals fought in the Red Army in World War 2 (eg the GDR's Hoffman and Poland's Jaruzelski). On a number of occasions they have shown a higher loyalty to the Soviets than to their own civilian governments. Just how effective these NSWP divisions would be once committed is another matter entirely. They are all conscript armies, and civilian unrest in eastern Europe might lead the Soviet marshals to place little trust in them. There might be deliberate attempts by NSWP governments to concentrate their most loyal troops into Joint Armed Forces — earmarked elements.

NSWP contingents in the Joint Armed Forces are thought to include both of East Germany's armies which are closely

integrated with the Group of Soviet Forces in Germany (GSFG). The Poles would probably assign their recently reorganised Silesian Tank Army. The Czechoslovak high-readiness 1st Army is also Joint Armed Forces-assigned. The actual degree of command integration between Soviet and NSWP units would be limited, usually following the Great Patriotic War pattern of placing armies under Soviet front commanders. It is possible that one of the Soviet divisions of the northern Group of Forces might be placed under the command of the Silesian Tank Army. Similarly the Baltic Fleet Naval Infantry Regiment might be involved in landings under the command of Poland's 7th Marine Division.

Fronts both with and without NSWP contingents would be grouped into theatres in war. Although some Soviet writings refer to theatres of war which encompass whole areas the size of Europe it is likely that the highest combined-arms command level is the Theatre of Military Operations (*Teatr Voyennykh Destviy*, or TVD). TVDs consist of a particular geographic area with its associated air and sea space. Some TVDs might in war be designated 'main' (or 'Glavny') theatres — GTVDs. A GTVD is the theatre in which the main strategic blow takes place. The Soviets have divided the world into a number of theatres including four ocean TVDs (OTVDs,) three inter-continental TVDs (related to strategic nuclear forces) and five continental ones.

The Red Army used theatre structures briefly in 1941 but they were soon bypassed as the Stavka preferred direct communication with the fronts. During the 1945 Manchurian operation a TVD HQ was established under Marshal Vasilevsky who wrote, 'Taking into account the remoteness of the Far Eastern Theatre of Operations from the centre, its vast area, difficult natural conditions, and also the need to make appropriate and timely use of the Soviet Pacific Fleet in suppport of all three fronts, the State Defence Committee set up a separate High Command for the strategic guidance of military operations'. Following the accession of Krushchev, during the 'massive retaliation' era, the Soviets concentrated on strategic nuclear planning, and the Ground Forces were not required to plan for sustained strategic land operations. Thus from the late 1940s to the late 1960s the TVD concept was forgotten and the front became the highest practical level of command.

The resurrection of TVDs began in 1968 when a special theatre HQ (the Danube High Command) was set up to direct the intervention in Czechoslovakia. Recently the Chief of the General Staff, Marshal Ogarkov, has shown a great deal of enthusiasm for

Left:
Commanders of the Russian, Polish and East German Baltic fleets confer with Adm Gorshkov during the 1968 'Sever' manoeuvres. The Combined Baltic Command of the WTO is in essence a permanently constituted theatre-level headquarters under a Soviet admiral. *Novosti*

Below left:
In recent years the East Germans have increasingly replaced the Poles as the most faithful Non-Soviet Pact member. They have acquired modern systems such as these SA-9 and SA-6 anti-aircraft missiles. *ADN*

Right:
East German forces practise river crossings. *Novosti*

Below right:
The 'front' or army group was the key level of command in the victory over Germany. These front colours hang today in Minsk.

them. He wrote in the July 1981 edition of the journal *Kommunist* 'It is not the front operation but the larger-scale form of operations — the strategic operation in the theatre of military operations — which should be regarded as the basic operation in a possible future war'. Prior to the outbreak of hostilities a *glavnokomanduyuschiye*, or commander-in-chief, will be appointed and assigned a staff which will be based on a sub-section of the General Staff Operations Main Directorate, in peacetime these staff groups (which are assigned to particular geographic areas) are constantly engaged in contingency planning for strategic operations. The war headquarters would include elements from the Navy, KGB, MVD, Strategic Rocket Forces and aviation elements as necessary.

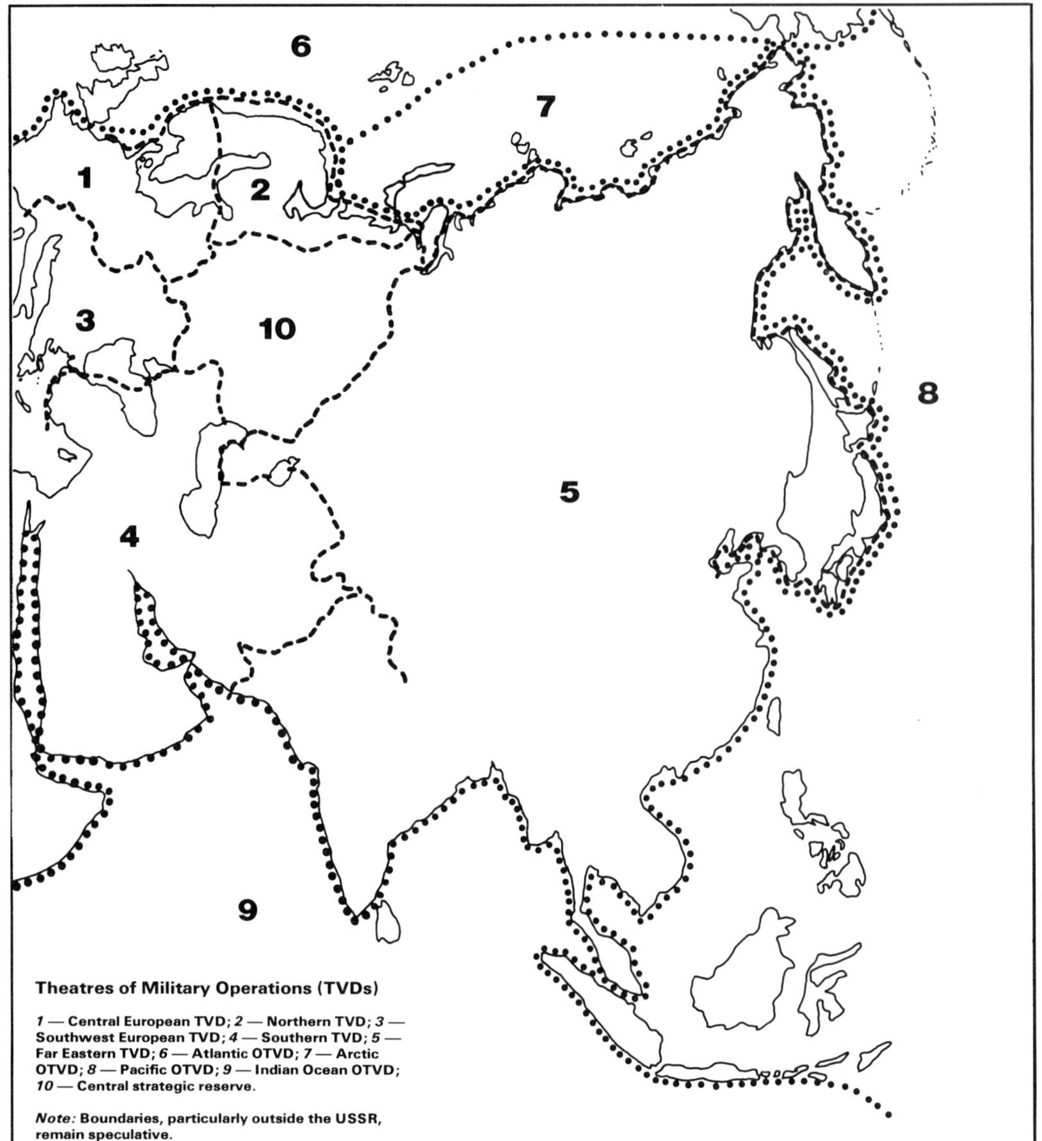

Theatres of Military Operations (TVDs)

1 — Central European TVD; *2* — Northern TVD; *3* — Southwest European TVD; *4* — Southern TVD; *5* — Far Eastern TVD; *6* — Atlantic OTVD; *7* — Arctic OTVD; *8* — Pacific OTVD; *9* — Indian Ocean OTVD; *10* — Central strategic reserve.

Note: Boundaries, particularly outside the USSR, remain speculative.

Below right:
During the early 1980s the Air Defence Forces were reorganised. Missiles, interceptors and radars have now been concentrated into a single organisation whose respective levels of command have exclusive responsibility for engaging intruders. *Novosti*

Below:
'Scaleboard' missiles are held for use at the front and theatre levels. *MoD*

Recent air forces restructuring reflects the shift in emphasis from fronts to theatres as the main focus of combined arms command. It is clear that the Soviets believe that all weapons must be unified at a level of command high enough to wage war throughout the enemy's operational and strategic depth. As Col Skovorodkin noted (*Military Thought*, February 1967), 'a major operation conducted in the TVD in fact at once encompasses its entire depth'. To do this the C-in-C has control of SS-20 missiles, Su-24 'Fencer' regiments, and all of the other necessary tools. He will use them to strike at enemy airfields, nuclear delivery means and reserves: 'combating strategic reserves in a theatre of military operations is an indispensable element of modern war' (Maj-Gen Kn. Dzelaukhov in *Military Thought*). The new theatre doctrine is one of the most important postwar developments in Military Art. It is worth examining the likely structure of TVDs and how they would operate in war.

Central European TVD

In peacetime the commander of GSFG holds the title 'commander-in-chief'. This man, currently Army-Gen Mikhail Zaytsev, would control three or four fronts (army groups). These might be constituted as follows:

Northern, or 1st German Front: 2nd Guards Tank Army, 3rd Shock Army, 20th Guards Army and GDR Military District V.
Central, or 2nd German Front: 1st Guards Tank Army, 8th Guards Army and GDR Military District III. This front might be based on the Northern Group of Forces HQ.
Southern, or Czechoslovak Front: the Soviet Central Group of Forces, CSSR 1st Army and elements from the Carpathian District.
A *fourth front* based on the Baltic or Byelorussian District HQ might include 5th Guards Tank Army, 7th Guards Tank Army (from the Byelorussian MD) or the 11th Guards Army (Baltic MD), and the Polish Silesian Tank Army.

In a war with the West this theatre would be designated a GTVD.

Southwest European TVD

This theatre would form the strategic grouping for any conflict in the Balkans or southern Europe. It is believed that it would be commanded by Army-Gen A. I. Gerasimov, a senior general and candidate member of the CPSU Central Committee. It would control a number of fronts based on the Southern Group of Forces, Odessa MD and Kiev MD headquarters. Troops from Hungary and Bulgaria would also be integrated. Armies from the Carpathian MD might be used if there was no conflict elsewhere in Europe.

Northern TVD

Any action on NATO's northern flank would be directed by this headquarters. It is debatable whether landings in the Baltic approaches would come under the aegis of this HQ, the Central European TVD, or indeed of a Baltic MTVD. The identity of the likely C-in-C is unknown.

Southern TVD

The evidence of the Afghanistan action is that Marshal Sokolev commands this theatre. Its principal forces consist of the Transcaucasus, Turkestan and possibly

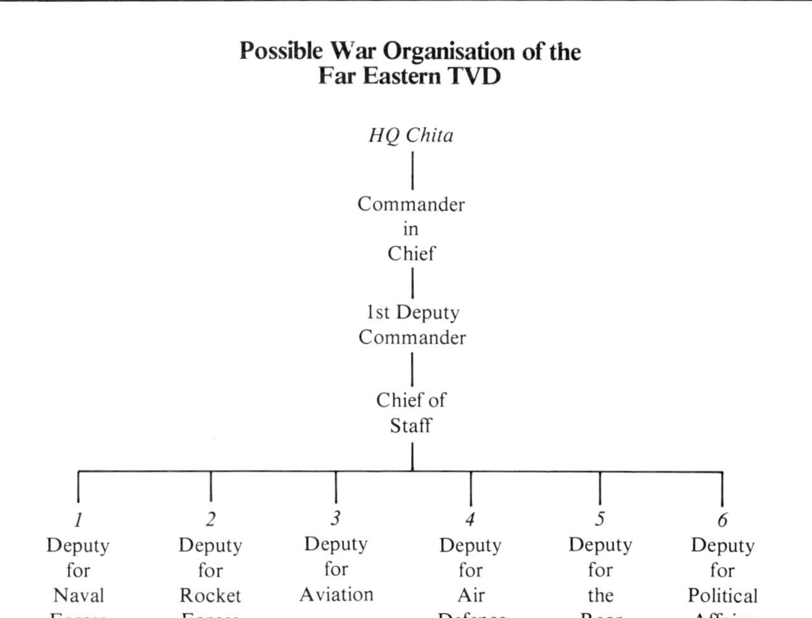

Forces available to Deputy Commanders
1 Coastal forces assigned from the Pacific Fleet including amphibious forces when needed. Large scale oceanic operations would fall under the Pacific OTVD.
2 A division of 90 Strategic Rocket Forces SS-20 missiles believed to be commanded from an HQ near Chita. Frontal 'Scaleboard' brigades might also fall under this commander.
3 30th Air Army of the AASU with its HQ in Irkutsk consisting of two Tu-22M 'Backfire' and three Su-24 'Fencer' regiments. The Far Eastern Air Force of Frontal Aviation with around 1,000 combat aircraft. Two airlift divisions of the VTA totalling 180 Il-76 'Candid' and An-12 'Cub' aircraft.

4 Far Eastern theatre PVO headquarters is believed to be in Novosibirsk and has control over interceptor aircraft, anti-aircraft missiles and radars within the theatre.
5 This deputy has command of a multitude of Rear Service, Railway, Pipeline Construction and Commandants Service units. He would also have control of perhaps a division of MVD Internal Troops and of detachments of Border Troops from the Eastern, Far Eastern, Transbaikal and Pacific frontier districts for rear security.

Ground Forces available to the C-in-C would include those stationed in the Siberian, Tranbaikal, and Far Eastern military districts and Mongolia.

Central Asian MDs and Soviet forces stationed in Afghanistan.

Far Eastern TVD

Army-Gen V. L. Govorov, the son of a celebrated wartime general, is currently C-in-C. In war he would command two or three fronts:

Far Eastern Front: three armies of the Far Eastern MD.
Transbaikal Front: two or more armies drawn from the Transbaikal MD and the Soviet garrison in Mongolia.
A *third front* might be formed from the Central Asian and Siberian MDs.

If the USSR found itself at war with China this would be designated a GTVD.

Fronts are not permanently constituted in peacetime. It is estimated that there are 16 likely frontal headquarters. These would be based on the four groups of forces, and the staffs of the larger military districts. Each front would command one or more armies and would have organic (ie dedicated) support that might include an artillery division, an air defence brigade and other support units.

Until recently the order of battle also included an air army of Frontal Aviation. These air armies have now been scrapped in favour of larger entities which correspond more closely to the theatres of military operations. However because TVDs (with the possible exception of the Central European one) do not function fully in peacetime the military district commands are responsible for day-to-day administrative support of Frontal Aviation and PVO regiments. It is interesting to note that the Central European TVD clearly has a theatre level aviation command structure. After the Czechoslovak operation three air armies (Nos 16 in northern CSFG, 24 in southern CSFG and 10 in Czechoslovakia) were all formed into a single HQ — 16 Air Army with 1,200 combat aircraft — much larger than any other air army. It is suspected that similar changes in the air forces assigned to the Far Eastern theatre took place early in the 1970s.

Selected military districts would be converted into fronts shortly before a war and their forces would be drawn predominantly but not entirely from the districts themselves. There would be some reallocation of armies and divisions between them. Those MDs

destined to become fronts in war combine two very important functions. In addition to sending an army group to war they must also mobilise the entire district to fight and survive the war. District headquarters elements responsible for conscription, civil defence, transport, construction and billeting, and pre-military training would not 'go to war' with the front HQ but would fulfil vital organisational missions in their areas of responsibility. The groups of forces HQs do not have these tasks and are in effect frontal command centres — although not officially. During a war frontal commanders would have responsibility for operations in their sectors (normally between 200 and 300km wide) and would set long range objectives. Evidently the re-emergence of TVDs in recent years has lessened the importance that frontal HQs would have in war. In some circumstances TVD commanders would bypass frontal HQs and exercise direct control over armies.

Armies are the highest peacetime combined arms command level. Armies may command two or more divisions, and have a variety of organic support including an artillery brigade and an air defence brigade.

There are 26 army HQs in the Soviet Army of which seven are tank armies. Generally speaking a tank army would have three tank and one motor rifle divisions, and a typical combined-arms army three motor rifle and one tank divisions. However there are no hard and fast rules: the army HQ at Boleslav for example commands one tank and one motor rifle division, and 40th Army in Kabul at one stage controlled seven motor rifle divisions. Armies are normally commanded by lieutenant-generals and are responsible for a frontage of between 40 and 80km depending on whether they are on the front's main or subsidiary axis of advance. The army commander is responsible for combat planning only two or three days ahead. It is quite likely that TVD commanders might retain one or more armies as theatre reserves. Theatre or front commanders might also designate entire armies as manoeuvre groups. These might be termed Operational Manoeuvre Groups with objectives of strategic importance.

It is also worth mentioning the six or seven identified corps HQs. A number of these are stationed in remote areas and serve to co-ordinate the activities of two or more divisions. They can be regarded as reserve army-level headquarters. In peacetime their organic support and manpower falls below that regarded as normal for armies but would be made up on mobilisation.

Having examined the theory and structure of Soviet command it is worth examining the technical means used for command and intelligence. Command signals are handled by army Signals Troops, the General Staff Communications Directorate, and the 8th Directorate of the KGB. Satellite, microwave, radio and land line links are all used. The Warsaw Pact has an important edge over the West in communications security (COMSEC) in that most of the armed forces can be reached by secure land lines. Nevertheless other forms of communication are used and according to US intelligence sources there are 75 hardened communications installations in the Moscow district alone.

Strategic and tactical communications accounted for 31% of Soviet military satellite launches in 1981-82. Strategic communications between command centres at the national level are handled by a constellation of eight Molniya satellites each with an average life of 750 days. These Molniya systems are placed into eccentric orbits in order to allow continuous coverage of the

USSR. Theatre needs are serviced by two constellations of tactical communications systems, one group of three orbiting in planes 120° apart, and another of 20-30 satellites in a single plane. An average life of 500 days means that the Soviets need to launch around 18 tactical communications systems per year. Because of its extensive network of secure land lines the USSR is a great deal less dependent on its satellite communications network than the USA and consequently its capabilities are modest. The use of satellite relays is of greatest significance in areas beyond the reach of the land line network. During the Afghan intervention for example (and before a land line was laid to Kabul) the 40th Army headquarters made extensive use of a Lolos ground station for satellite contact with the Kremlin. It is believed that Air Defence Troops sent to Syria in summer 1983 are integrated into the USSR air defence command network by this means. Use of airborne command posts is also common; there are believed to be several Il-62 and Il-76 aircraft configured for use by national leaders. An-12 transports have been observed in a tactical command role in Afghanistan, and it is also reported that a number of Mil-6 helicopters serve in this role in GSFG.

The massive amount of information flowing through high-level HQs has forced the Soviets to give increasing attention to computers. Marshal Ogarkov has noted that there is 'an increasing amount of work to be accomplished by the organs of strategic leadership while the time to accomplish it is being reduced'. Computers of the Ryad 1, 2 and 3 series have been introduced into high level command centres, particularly of the PVO and Strategic Rocket Forces. Success in this field has encouraged them to experiment with computers at the operational/tactical level in troop control. Marshal of Signal Troops A. I. Belov states 'use of automatic systems is the main trend in improving troop control' (*Soviet Military Review*, 4/80).

The importance of mathematical norms in Soviet planning makes the use of computers particularly convenient. Norms stipulate everything from the number of kilometres a division should advance in given conditions to the number of artillery rounds required to destroy an enemy position. The Russians believe that computers will free their commander from a great deal of work in any future conflict. However, the introduction of computers at army level presents many problems, not least the hitherto modest capabilities of the Soviet computer industry. With army and divisional HQs moving once a day the computers would have to be extremely rugged, and some time would have to be spent in each new location stabilising the system. During a rapid advance there will be no time to lay land lines, and the machinery would be dependent on conventional radio links.

Soviet attempts to maintain their own communications will be accompanied by measures to disrupt enemy communications. Maj-Gen N. Vasendin and Col N. Kuznetsov point out that 'high altitude nuclear explosions can be carried out in the beginning and in the course of the war to destroy the system of control and communications'. Such nuclear bursts (to create an electro-magnetic pulse, or EMP as it is known in the West) would affect Warsaw Pact communications as well. Aircraft could be used to drop huge quantities of chaff (strips of metal foil) to disrupt radars and radios, and this was done during the Czech operation, when the Russians also used a jamming system so large that is was carried in a train. Signals interception regiments are organic to fronts and interception battalions to armies. Their mission is to eavesdrop on enemy communications, whereas front and army Radio-Electronic Combat battalions are responsible for disrupting them. NATO is well aware of the EW threat, and in 1980 during Exercise 'Crusader' the 1st British Corps successfully deployed to battle positions in radio silence.

Use of interception units is important in compromising enemy COMSEC. In recent years signals intelligence (SIGINT) has become the most important means of intelligence gathering. Monitoring of signals traffic can give warning of impending attack, allow for timely updating of the enemy order of battle, and also indicate weak points. Warsaw Pact SIGINT capabilities are extensive, ranging from field units to intelligence gathering trawlers at sea and 'ferret' aircraft such as the An-12 'Cub-B' and Il-18 'Coot-A'. Aircraft are also equipped for the electronic intelligence (ELINT) role using sideways looking radar, infra-red line scan, and other devices capable of detecting troop movements. Responsibility for processing SIGINT rests with the KGB 8th Directorate, and General Staff Intelligence Main Directorate (GRU), which also has 'in-house' SIGINT analysis.

Increasingly sophisticated satellites are being employed in the ELINT and photo-reconnaissance roles. In 1981-82 launches of such systems accounted for 41% of the Soviets' military space activity. During the Yom Kippur War they orbited seven photo-reconnaissance satellites each of which had a mission of only around $5\frac{1}{2}$ days before recovery. The ability to return information to earth by capsule without bringing the whole system back has only been acquired recently and new 'spies in the sky' have orbital lives of around 30 days. Even so the seemingly very high launch rate (about 35 per year) is only enough to maintain two simultaneously operational units. Presumably these are tasked to observe US stratetic nuclear forces rather than to provide commanders with battlefield intelligence. A six-satellite constellation is maintained for ELINT purposes giving information on hostile signals traffic radars and countermeasures. Battlefield tactical photo-reconnaissance will therefore be carried out predominantly by aircraft.

Human intelligence (HUMINT) can be provided by networks of agents already in place in West Germany and other countries. Intelligence troops, long range reconnaissance, airborne and raiding forces might also be used to supplement this shortly before and following the outbreak of hostilities. According to Western intelligence sources Soviet SAS-type troops are sometimes sent into the West (as long distance lorry drivers, or under another cover) to have a closer look at the targets they would be sent to attack in war. Their missions would include sabotage and the assassination of important military/political figures as well as reconnaissance.

3. THE MUSCLE

THE ORDER OF BATTLE

The efficiency of Soviet forces in any possible war will be determined largely by their peacetime combat readiness and standards of training. Soviet Army divisions are divided into four types: *razvertavie* (combat ready), *polurazvertavie* (semi-ready), *uchebnaya* (training) and *kadirovannye* (cadre). The establishment of men and equipment varies widely between these types of formation. *Razvertavie* corresponds to the Western classification of Soviet readiness category I, *kadirovannye* to category III, some semi-ready and training divisions are category II, and others category III. Category I forma-tions are maintained at 75-100% of strength and would be ready for war at very short notice. Category II divisions have nearly all of their equipment stocks but only half to three-quarters of their manpower. The lowest readiness formations are the category III ones manned at only 10-30% strength and are often short of combat equipment.

In or shortly before the outbreak of a war the empty places in these category II and III divisions would be filled with recalled reservists. The Ground Forces alone demobilise 700,000 men a year so something like 3,500,000 have completed service in the

Right:
The forward based groups of forces are maintained at the highest readiness. This competition between Russian and East German signallers is the only type of outside contact available to many members of the Soviet garrison in East Germany. *ADN*

last five years. There are a number of practical problems which prevent the Soviets from using this pool of manpower to its full potential. Within the low readiness units manpower is spread throughout with say just one man manning a tank. There can be very little realistic combat training for either officers or enlisted men, leading to low standards. When mobilised these cadre units would receive reservists who in all likelihood would have done their military service years previously in a different area of the country, with different equipment. Unlike the reserve forces of many Western countries these reservists do not train regularly as vehicle crews and sections with the units that they would join in war. Much of the hardware in cadre divisions is obsolete: some of the divisions that entered Afghanistan had artillery which dated from World War 2, and others have tanks of a similar vintage.

A Soviet tank captain who later defected to the West where he writes under the pseudonym Viktor Suvorov has described the appalling standards of readiness in these cadre divisions just prior to 1968 intervention in Czechoslovakia: 'There were only 12 men in a company: the commander of the company, a captain, and 10 drivers. At mobilisation all the missing members, gunners, loaders, tank commanders, even the company sergeant/majors and the platoon commanders came from the reservists'. He goes on to describe the attempts to ready the mobilised formation for action. 'After four months of training only one tank battalion in seven ... was accepted as being ready for battle. If war had started then the division would not of course had four months, training but only one or two weeks maximum. It would have been thrown into battle and would have been destroyed' (Viktor Suvorov *The Liberators*). Even today (and the evidence of the Afghan operation is that there has been little improvement in the situation) category III divisions would take months to prepare for war, and they must be considered separately in calculations of Soviet power. Talk of the Soviet Army's 174 divisions is highly deceptive because over half of the motor rifle divisions which make up the bulk of the total are category III skeleton formations. The readiness of war of these *kadirovannye* divisions is far lower than that of the British Territorial Army or US National Guard Reserve brigades which are usually excluded from calculations of Western strength. If Soviet, and other Non-Soviet Warsaw Pact, category III formations are excluded from the total of regular Pact forces, or Western reserves included, the ratio of forces looks considerably more balanced.

In order to prepare the reserve formations in the western military districts for a general European war the Soviets would need to call up at least 206,000 men (75% of the strength of 25 divisions), and when one includes support formations the figure would exceed 300,000 just for the Ground Forces. A great many civilian vehicles registered with the local military district headquarters under the *autokolomka* system would be needed to augment transport capacity. Once mobilised the units would need time for training and deployment. All of this would take months and would present obvious signals to the Western intelligence services. For this reason the Soviet Army would find it near impossible to conduct this mobilisation undetected and it would lose the all-important factor of surprise. Similarly half of the NSWP formations which are also cadre strength could not be mobilised without alerting NATO intelligence. According to one of the West's most celebrated experts on Russian military power, Professor John Erickson, such a mobilisation 'must run counter to the surprise factor which is a primary element of Soviet military doctrine and practice'.

These cadre divisions do however have their uses. On the Chinese border and in other remote areas they allow the Russians to keep equipment and organisation in place ready for activation in time of crisis. In any prolonged war the cadre divisions could replace those in the front line which had been decimated by conventional or nuclear strikes. This is acknowledged by Maj-Gen Dzhelaukhov, a General Staff strategist; 'extensive destruction and heavy losses resulting from the use of nuclear weapons will disrupt the system of operational organisation of troops in several theatres of military operations or strategic sectors', and he adds 'the fast-moving nature of the development of offensive operations causes sharp changes in the situation, which in turn make it necessary to bring large strategic as well as operational reserves into the battle'.

Of course many of the formations located in the western military districts are higher readiness category II and I units. These would be available to move to the front even before the outbreak of hostilities, although not without a massive logistics operation. The constraints of geography and readiness

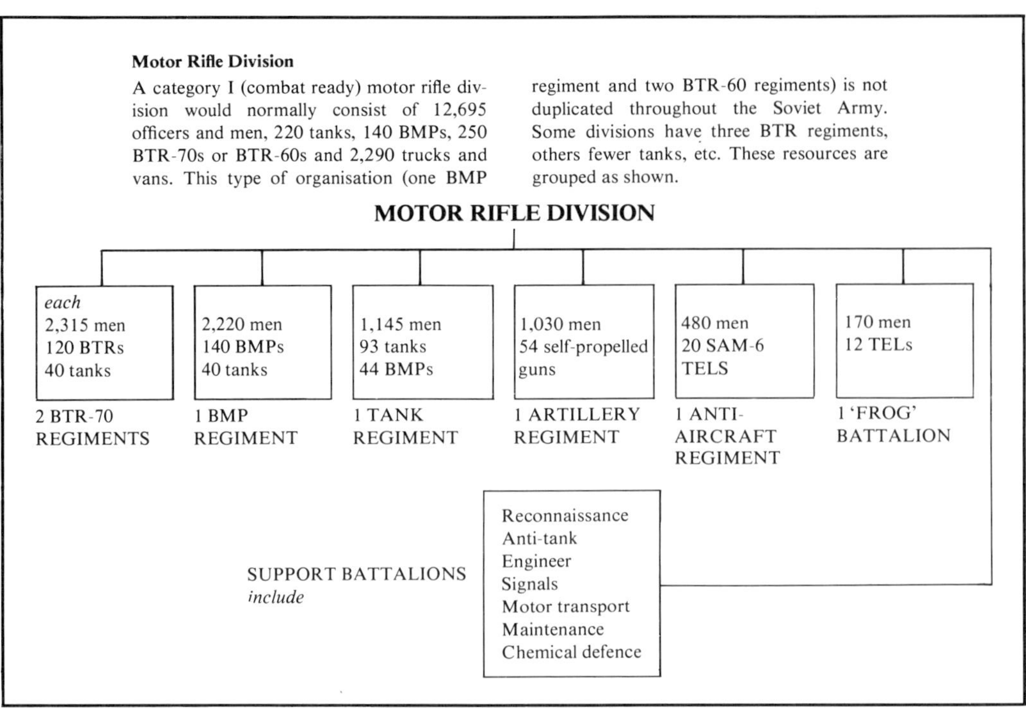

effectively divide the Soviet Army into three strategic echelons. The first consists of the groups of forces and selected NSWP elements which would be ready for combat at a moment's notice, the second of high readiness formations in the western USSR which could be transferred to the battle area relatively quickly, and lastly the category III formations forming the third strategic echelon. It would have the greatest chance of maintaining surprise if it committed only the first echelon.

At the end of the Great Patriotic War the Red Army had over 500 rifle divisions and about a tenth that number of tank formations. Their experience of war gave the Russians such faith in tank forces that since then the number of tank divisions has remained virtually unchanged whereas the wartime infantry force has been cut by two-thirds. When one considers that since the motorisation of the rifle divisions these too have also had large numbers of tanks, then the Soviet obsession with armour becomes apparent. Following the war many divisions were brought back to the USSR and many more disbanded, and the system of military districts were established for the peacetime administration of the Army.

The history of most of the divisions in the Soviet Army today can be traced back to World War 2, and some to the 1918-21 Civil War. Many have honorary titles awarded for participation in particular battles and campaigns. Some of these titles such as 'Vitebsk' and 'Smolensk' were awarded to many divisions, others are unique. Soviet open source literature almost always refers to formations by these titles rather than by their number — hence the Taman Guards Motor Rifle Division is almost never called the 2nd Guards. The actual number of divisions that carry these honorific titles is unknown, but during the war it did not exceed 40% according to German intelligence documents. Of these honorifics a small number are regularly singled out for mentions in Soviet periodicals. The formations accorded this treatment are the Taman, Rogachev, Chapaev, Panfilov, and Moscow-Minsk Guards Motor Rifle, the Samara-Ulyanovsk Motor Rifle, the Kantemirov and Ural Volunteers Guards Tank, and the Chernigov Guards Air Assault divisions. These formations are held up as models for 'socialist emulation' by the officers and soldiers of other units out of the public eye. The Soviet defector Viktor Suvorov refers to them as the 'court' divisions, and they also participate in the annual 7 November parades held in Moscow's Red Square and in other military districts around the country.

The 'Guards' title is an honorary one, the first four guards divisions being so named on 18 September 1941. By the end of the war the guards title had been given to 11 all-arms armies, six tank armies and 117 infantry divisions. Today there are around 80 tank, motor rifle, and air assault guards divisions, most of which are stationed in the groups of forces or the western Soviet Union. Soldiers serving in these units are known as 'guard-

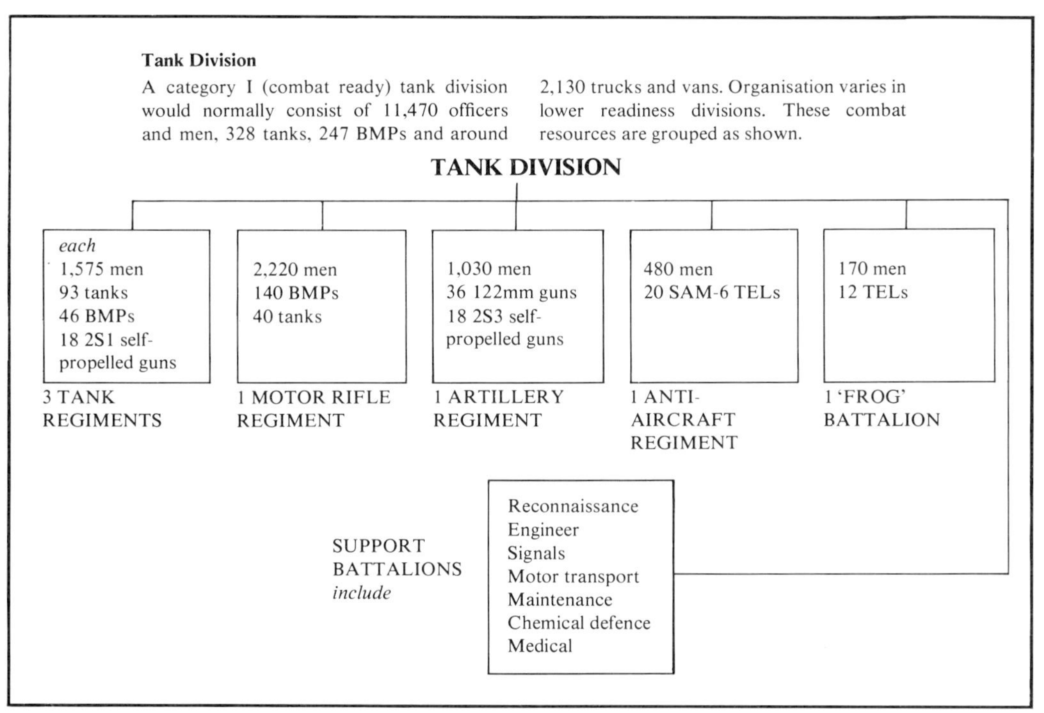

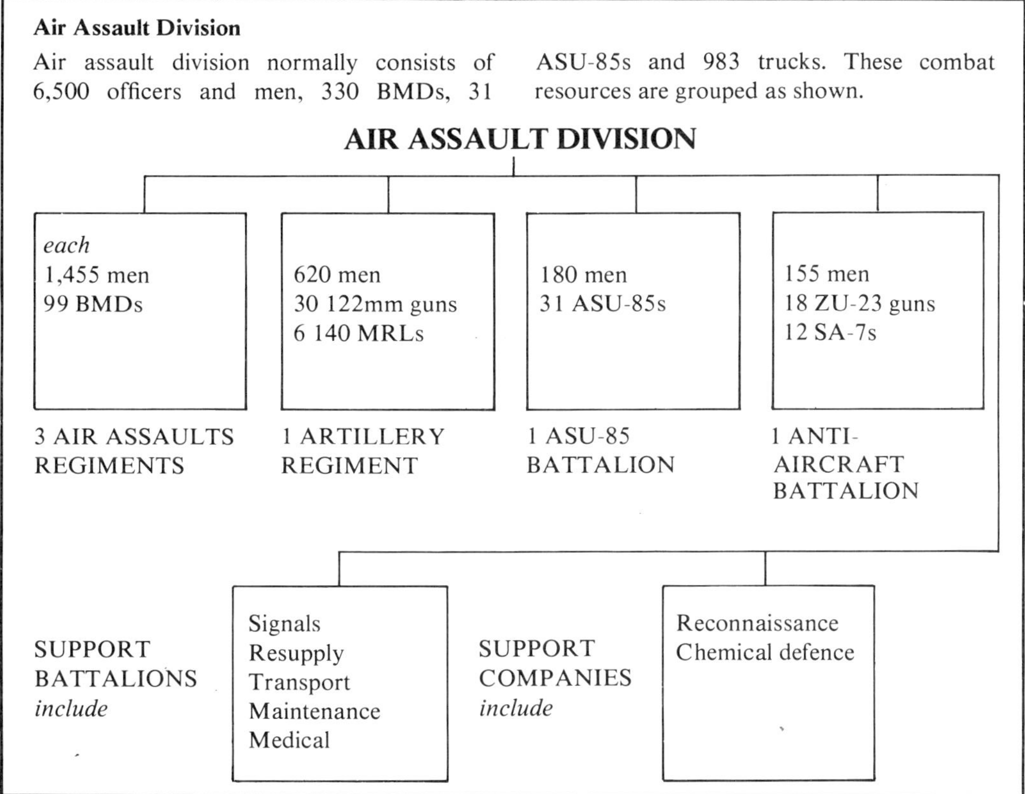

smen' and keep this title even when posted to other units. There does not appear to be any great difference in professionalism between between guards and other formations; indeed in GSFG the majority of formations have this title. In the more remote districts where there are only one or two guards divisions (eg in the Transcaucasus and Central Asian MDs) it is possible that they maintain higher standards.

A number of military collectives have been awarded decorations, and these are pinned to the colours becoming a part of the unit's honorific. The oldest among them, dating from 1918, is the Order of the Red Banner which has been given to many field units as well as most of the military districts. The Order of Lenin ranks higher, and like the others can be awarded to individuals too.

A careful study of open Soviet sources and

Artillery Division

The so-called 'Type A' artillery division is assigned to front commanders. Some widely differing organisational structures exist. 'Type B' artillery divisions have 162 guns and would be assigned to army or front commanders. The typical 'Type A' formation would have 324 field pieces, 6,750 officers and men and 1,300 trucks and vans grouped as shown.

ARTILLERY DIVISION

each
1,050 men
54 130mm
guns (possibly
being replaced
by 2S5 152mm
SPGs)

each
1,050 men
54 152mm
howitzers

c300 men
c36 100mm
anti-tank
guns

Various

3 ARTILLERY
REGIMENTS
(130mm)

3 ARTILLERY
REGIMENTS
(152mm)

1 ANTI-TANK
BATTALION

1 ANTI-AIRCRAFT
BATTALION

SUPPORT
BATTALIONS
include

Target acquisition
Motor transport
Maintenance

SUPPORT
COMPANIES
include

Ordnance
Ammunition handling

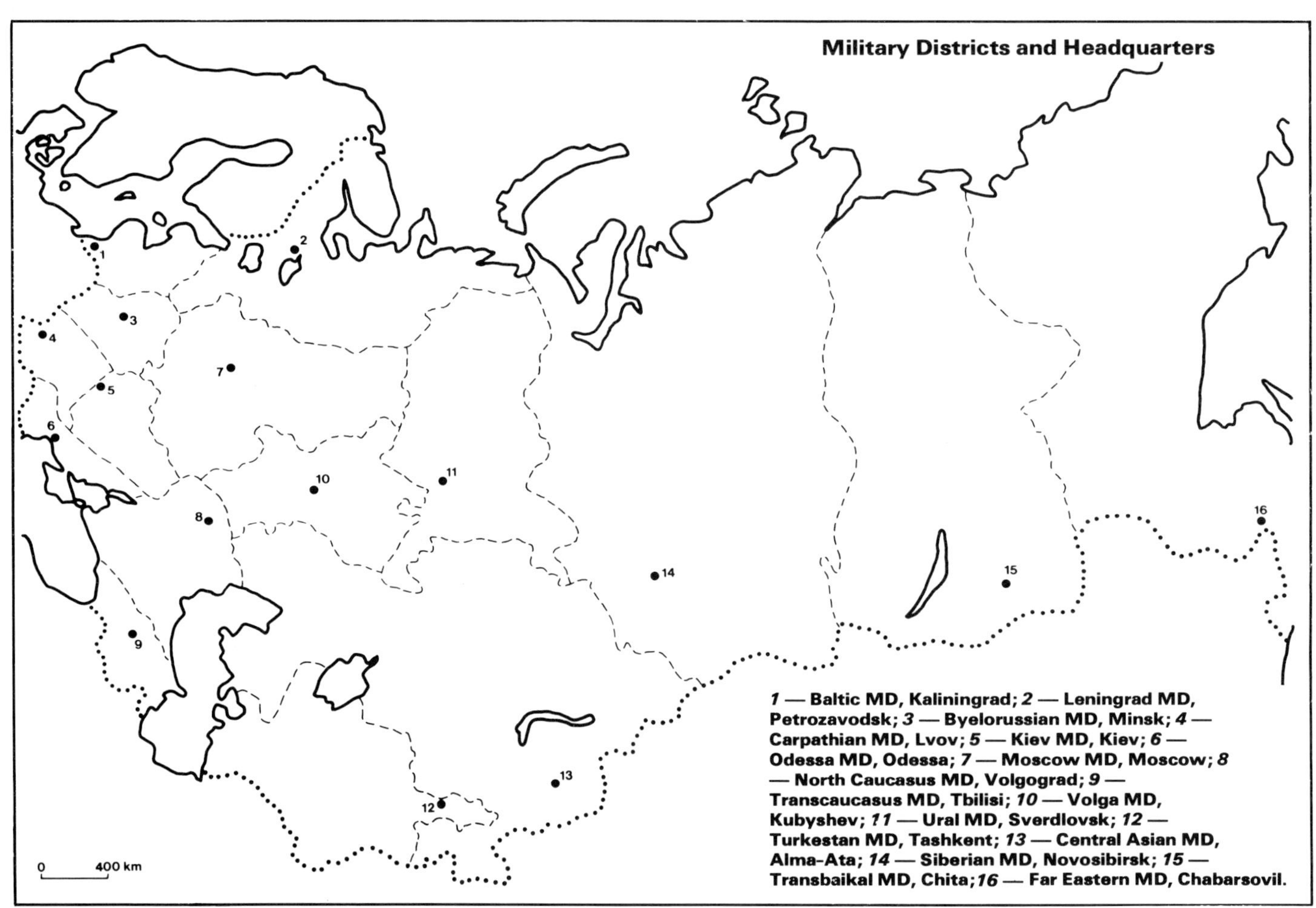

Military Districts and Headquarters

1
2
3
4
5
6
7
8
9
10
11
12
13
14
15
16

0   400 km

1 — Baltic MD, Kaliningrad; 2 — Leningrad MD, Petrozavodsk; 3 — Byelorussian MD, Minsk; 4 — Carpathian MD, Lvov; 5 — Kiev MD, Kiev; 6 — Odessa MD, Odessa; 7 — Moscow MD, Moscow; 8 — North Caucasus MD, Volgograd; 9 — Transcaucasus MD, Tbilisi; 10 — Volga MD, Kubyshev; 11 — Ural MD, Sverdlovsk; 12 — Turkestan MD, Tashkent; 13 — Central Asian MD, Alma-Ata; 14 — Siberian MD, Novosibirsk; 15 — Transbaikal MD, Chita; 16 — Far Eastern MD, Chabarsovil.

use of information published indirectly by Western intelligence agencies allows us to build up an accurate picture of the order of battle and deployment of the Soviet Army. Of course there are areas of doubt, particularly concerning dispositions on the Chinese border where forces were doubled during the 1960s and 1970s. Within the groups of forces where all forces are combat ready there is an established relationship between armies and their subordinate divisions and they have been listed accordingly. In the military districts forces have been listed in the order air assault, tank, motor rifle and artillery and in overall order of readiness.

Above:
GSFG. This guards tank regiment carries the honorific 'Suche Bator' received for taking part in the brief Russo–Japanese War of 1938. In the foreground are T–62 tanks, the unit's main fighting power; behind them are BMPs of the motor rifle battalion, 2S1 self-propelled guns and other support elements. *ADN*

Group of Soviet Forces in Germany

HQ: Zossen-Wunsdorff, German Democratic Republic

1st Guards Tank Army	Dresden
9 Tk Div 'Bobruisk'	Riesa/Sachsen-Zeithan
11 Gds Tk Div, 'Carpathian-Berlin'	Dresden
20 Gds MR Div 'Carpathian'	Grimma

2nd Guards Tank Army	Furstenburg
9 Gds Tk Div 'Uman-Vistula'	Neustrelitz
32 Gds MR Div 'Azerbaijan-Taman-Sevastopol'	Perleberg
94 Gds MR Div 'Zvenigorodok-Pommerania-Berlin,	Schwerin
207 MR Div 'Pommerania-Berlin'	Stendal

3rd Shock Army	Magdeburg
10 Gds Tk Div 'Ural Volunteers-Lvov', named after MSU R. I. Malinovski	Krampnitz
12 Gds Tk Div 'Uman'	Neuruppin
7 Gds Tk Div 'Kiev-Berlin'	Dessau
47 Gds Tk Div 'Dnepropetrovsk-Smolensk'	Hillersleben

8th Guards Army	Nohra
79 Gds Tk Div	Jena
27 Gds MR Div 'Korsun-Novobugin'	Halle
39 Gds MR Div 'Barvenkovo-Posen'	Ohrduf
57 Gds MR Div 'Smolensk-Stalingrad-Krivoi Rog-Kharkov'	Naumberg

20th Guards Army	Ebersvald
25 Tk Div 'Novgorod-Volynsk'	Templin/Vogelsang
32 Gds Tk Div	Juterborg
6 Gds MR Div 'Rovno-Lvov'	Bernau
19 Gds MR Div 'Slonim-Pommerania'	Doberitz

Centrally held troops	
34 Gds Arty Div	Potsdam
? Air Asslt Bde	Cottbus
? Special Forces Brigade	Neuruppin

Clearly GSFG is the most powerful striking force in the ground forces, and its headquarters would become that of the Central GTVD in war, if it is not already, as well as providing a front HQ. Most of its units were involved in the final stages of the last war, which is reflected in their honorifics. A treaty between the USSR and East Germany signed on 20 September 1955 formalised the Soviet presence. The high readiness (all category I) of these forces provides the most convincing rationale for Western conventional defence in Central Europe, for they could go to war with the minimum of delay. East Germany's forces are incorporated into GSFG in peacetime and would remain so in war. The term 'Shock Army' is an honorary one; five were created during the war, but only the 3rd has survived. GSFG was reorganised in 1982-83; this table includes those changes. The main trend was that 20th Guards Army received more armour (perhaps it will revert to its former designation, 4th Guards Tank Army), and that the 1st Guards Tank Army lost two of its tank divisions.

Central Group of Forces

HQ: Molovice, Czechoslovakia

? Army	Boleslav
18 Gds MR Div 'Smolensk'	Mlada-Boleslav
31 Tk Div	Milovice
? Army	Olomouc
51 Tk Div	Bruntal

Above:
CGF. The forces of the Central Group are well equipped for mobile operations. *Novosti*

55 Gds MR Div 'Irkutsk-Pinsk named after RSFSR Supreme Soviet'
                    Vysoke Myoto
30 Gds MR Div   Zvolen

The presence of the CGF in Czechoslovakia dates back only to 1968 when it was formed from elements of the Byelorussian and Carpathian districts involved in the intervention in that country. In war the CGF could provide a front composed of two Soviet and one Czech army for the Central European TVD. Between 1978 and 1983 the CGF had four different commanders, an unusual turnover for the Soviets.

Northern Group of Forces
HQ: Leignica, Poland
   20 Tk Div   Borne
   38 Tk Div   Swietoszow

The war role of the NGF headquarters remains something of a mystery. It probably provides a second frontal command centre for the forces of GSFG. It is suspected that the 20th Tank Division would serve under the 20th Guards Army, and the 38th Tank Division under the Polish tank army. Alternatively these divisions might join one of the tank armies of the Byelorussian district. Early in the 1980s what was the 37th Air Army of Frontal Aviation became the 24th Air Army of a new organisation, Aviation Armies of the Soviet Union — a theatre-level strike force for central Europe. The NGF has been constantly reduced in strength from a postwar high of 300,000 men in 1947 to today's total of 40,000.

Southern Group of Forces
HQ: Budapest-Matysafold, Hungary
   2 Tk Div   Esztergom
5 Tk Div   Vezszprem
35 Gds MR Div 'Losovaya'   Kecskemet
102 Gds MR Div 'Novgorod-Seversk-Pomerania'   Szekeshervar

The small category I forces of the SGF could be supplemented by forces for the Kiev and Odessa military districts. This headquarters might also command in war an army of Hungarian troops as well as one formed from its own units.

Baltic Military District
HQ: Kalinigard
11th Guards Army   Kaliningrad
   7 Gds Air Asslt Div (cat I) 'Cherkassy'
                   Kaunas
   1 Tk Div (cat I) 'Unecha'   Kalinigrad
   44 Gds Air Asslt Div (cat II)   Jonava
   40 Gds Tk Div (cat II)   Sovetsk
   25 Gds Tk Div (cat II)   Dobele
   1 Gds MR Div (cat II) 'Proletarian Moscow-Minsk'   Kaliningrad
   149 (?) Arty Div   Kaliningrad
   (?) 344 Arty Div   Kaliningrad
   3 Gds MR Div (cat III) 'Volnovkha-Evpatoriya'   Klaipeda
   56 Gds MR Div (cat III) 'Smolensk named after A. Matrosov'   Tallinn
   107 MR Div (cat III) 'Stry-Stanislav-Drokobycz-Borislav'   Vilnus
   26 Gds MR Div (cat III) 'Eastern Siberia-Chernyakov-Gudorov'   Gusev
   16 MR Div (cat III)   Jonava

This district provides an important back-up force for the central European theatre, and possibly the northern theatre as well. Its headquarters in Kaliningrad is one of the largest garrison towns in the USSR, and coincidentally it was the 11th Guards Army which provided the bulk of the force which liberated the town from the Nazis.

Byelorussian Military District
HQ: Minsk
5th Guards Tank Army   Bobruisk
7th Guards Tank Army   Borisov
28th Army   Grodno
   103 Gds Air Asslt Div (cat I)   Vitebsk
   8 Gds Tk Div (cat I) 'Zaporozhe-Nikopol-Lublin'   Maryina-Gorka
   6 Gds Tk Div (cat I) 'Kiev-Fastov'   ?
   120 Gds MR Div (cat I) 'Rogachev-Bialystock named after BSSR Supreme Soviet'   Minsk
   3 Gds Tk Div (cat II) 'Kotelnikovo'   Lepel
   8 (?) Tk Div (cat II)   Slonim
   22 Tk Div (cat II)   Bobruisk

29 Tk Div (cat II) 'Kirovograd-Znamenka'	Slutsk
34 Tk Div (cat II)	Borisov
37 Gds Tk Div (cat II)	Polotsk
47 Tk Div (cat II)	Borisov
? MR Div (cat II)	Borisov
3 Gds Arty Div 'Vitebsk'	Osipovici
50 Gds MR Div (cat III) 'Baranovich-Nikopol-Stalino'	Brest

The tank heavy forces of the Byelorussian MD form a powerful exploitation force for operations in Europe. By 1945 there were four Byelorussian fronts and some of the forces from them were formed into this district. A number of the divisions currently subordinated to 5th Guards Tank Army and 28th Army served under these headquarters during the war. 7th Guards Tank Army and some of the district's tank formations are postwar creations.

Carpathian Military District
HQ: Lvov

8th Guards Tank Army	Zhitomir
13th Army	Rovno
38th Army	Ivano-Frankovsk
23 Tk Div (cat I) 'Vienna-Zhitomir'	Ovruch
15 Gds MR Div (cat I) 'Kharkov'	Vladimir-Volinski
13 Tk Div (cat II)	Novograd-Volinski
24 MR Div (cat II) 'Samara-Ulyanovsk-Berdichev Iron'	Lvov
117 Gds Tk Div (cat II)	Berdichev
128 Gds MR Div (cat II) 'Carpathian-Turkestan'	Mukachevo
161 MR Div (cat II) 'Novorossiisk'	Uzhgorod
81 Arty Div	Vinogradow
26 Arty Div	Kamenskaya-Bugskaya
17 MR Div (cat III) 'Bobruisk-Moskvorezsk'	Khmeinitsky
66 Gds MR Div (cat III) 'Poltava'	Chernovisty
97 Gds MR Div (cat III) 'Poltava'	Slavuta
70 Gds MR Div (cat III) 'Gluckhov-Lvov'	Isyaslav (?)

Many of the formations that serve under this commander belonged to the Ukranian fronts during the war, and they were associated with the liberation of many towns in the district. Its forces played an important role in the 1968 Czechoslovak crisis. One of its two artillery divisions may be earmarked to reinforce the Central Group of Forces.

Kiev Military District
HQ: Kiev

1st Guards Army	Chernigov
3rd (?) Guards Tank Army	Dnepepetrovsk
18 Gds Tk Div (cat II)	Cherkassy
20 Gds Tk Div (cat II)	Krivoi-Rog
42 Gds Tk Div (cat II)	Volnoye
75 Gds Tk Div (cat II)	Chuguyev
41 Gds Tk Div (cat II)	Atemovsk
14 (?) Tk Div (cat II)	Vypolozov
287 MR Div (cat III) 'Novgorod-Volinsk'	Volnoye
72 Gds MR Div (cat III) 'Krasnograd'	Belaya-Tserkov
4 MR Div (cat III)	Lugansk a/o Voroshilovgrad
25 Gds MR Div (cat III) 'Budapest-Sinelnikov named after V. T. Chapaev'	Lubny
? Arty Div	Novomoskovsk
? Arty Div	Fastov

The Kiev along with the Byelorussian and Carpathian districts is one of the most important depots of the Soviet Army. Its tank heavy forces could provide follow up forces for operations in southwestern Europe.

Odessa Military District
HQ: Odessa

19th Army	Kishinev
? Corps	Simferopol
102 Gds Air Asslt Div (cat I) 'Svir-Petrozavodsk'	Kishinev
59 Gds MR Div (cat II) 'Kramatorok-	

Left:
Odessa MD. Naval infantrymen of the Black Sea Fleet are based in the district. This unit might be used to secure the outlet to the Mediterranean or sent to some Middle Eastern trouble spot.
Tass

Nikopol-Stalino'	Tirasopol
92 MR Div (cat II)	Nikolayev
128 MR Div (cat II)	Feodisiya
2 Gds Arty Div	Zaporozhe
98 Gds MR Div (cat III)	Bolgrad
126 MR Div (cat III) 'Gorlovka'	
	Simferopol
286 MR Div (cat III) 'Leningrad'	
	Odessa

This command would provide the bulk of the rifle divisions for an operation in the southwestern theatre. It is interesting to speculate what attitude the Rumanians would take to the passage of these forces across their country, perhaps on their way to a war with Greece or Turkey, as for the last 15 years they have refused to have Soviet troops on their territory. Doubtless the General Staff has a plan for dealing with this contingency.

North Caucasus Military District
HQ: Rostov

? Corps	Krasnodar
? Corps	Volgograd
? Tk Div (cat II)	Novocherkassk a/o
	Urypinsk

4 Arty Div	Buynaksk a/o Mikhachkala
9 MR Div (cat III)	Maykop
19 MR Div (cat III)	Orzhonikidzye
24 Gds MR Div (cat III) 'Aleksandriya'	Crozny
73 MR Div (cat III) 'Slonim-Luninets-Novosybkov-Zhlobin'	Novorossiysk
266 MR Div (cat III) 'Artemosk'	Volgograd

These forces form a reserve for employment in southwest Europe or the Southern TVD. It is a low readiness district with its army level HQs maintained only as corps staffs.

Leningrad Military District

HQ: Petrozavdonsk

6th Army	Petrozavdonsk
? Corps	Vyborg
? Corps	Archangel
76 Gds Air Asslt Div (cat I) 'Cernigov-Brest Litovsk-Kovel-Elnya'	P'skov
37 Gds MR Div (cat I) 'Rezhitsa'	Pargolova
2 Gds Tk Div (cat II) 'Tatsin'	Leningrad
314 MR Div (cat II) 'Kingisepp-Petsamo'	Kandalaksha
45 Gds MR Div (cat III)	Vyborg
45 MR Div (cat III) 'Kirkenes'	Murmansk a/o Pechenga
64 Gds MR Div (cat III) 'Krasnoe Selo-Mogilev-Vyborg'	Priozorsk
77 Gds MR Div (cat III) 'Chernigov-Kalinkovich'	Iskagorka a/o Archangel
111 Gds MR Div (cat III)	Sortavala
69 MR Div (cat III) 'Sevsk-Slonim-Luninets'	Vologda

These forces would form the basis of the Northern TVD and would take part in actions on NATO's northern flank. It is believed that 45 and 314 Motor Rifle Divisions are earmarked for an assault on Norway, and they are specially equipped for operations in arctic areas.

Moscow Military District

HQ: Moscow

106 Gds Air Asslt Div (cat I) 'Dnieper-Transbaikal'	Tula
2 Gds MR Div (cat I) 'Taman named after after M. I. Kalinin'	Alabino
? Gds MR Div (cat I)	Tambov
4 Gds Tk Div (cat II) 'Kantemirov-Shepetova' 'named after Yuri Andropov'	Naro-Fominsk
15 Gds Tk Div (cat II)	Gorkiy a/o Kovrov
13 MR Div (cat III)	Kovrov a/o Kursk
32 Gds MR Div (cat III)	Kalinin

Formations in this district have important public duties as well as military training. The Kantemirov division is credited with saving the Politburo from a coup by Stalin's security chief Beria following the leader's death in 1953.

Ural Military District

HQ: Sverdlovsk

? Tk Div (cat II)	Kamyshlov
77 MR Div (cat III)	Sverdlovsk
? MR Div (cat III)	Chebarku

This district would not form a front in war.

Volga Military District

HQ: Kubishev

21 MR Div (cat III) 'Perm'	Totskoye
43 MR Div (cat III)	Kubishev
96 MR Div (cat III) 'Gomel-Slonim-Luninets'	Kazan
? Arty Div	Totskoye

Like the Ural MD this would not form a frontal HQ in war.

Transcaucasus Military District
HQ: Tbilisi
76th Guards Army   Yerevan
4th Army   Baku
45th Army   Kutaisi
   104 Gds Air Asslt Div (cat I)   Kirovobad
   6 MR Div 'Orel-Tolbukhin'   Lenkoran
   10 MR Div   Akhalkalaki
   11 (?) MR Div   Akhalkalaki
   31 Gds MR Div 'Vitebsk-Dukhovshchina-
     Kovno'   Kirovobad
   26 MR Div   Kirovakan
   75 MR Div   Nakhichevan a/o Dzul'fa
   164 MR Div 'Vitebsk'   Yerevan
   216 MR Div   Baku
   261 MR Div 'Armenia-Erevan-
     Dukhovshchina'   Leninakan
   414 MR Div 'Anara-Georgia'   Batumi
   ? MR Div   Tbilisi
   ? Arty Div   Kutaisi

The Transcaucasus command is the most important in the Southern TVD which would provide forces for operations against Turkey or Iran. Three of the MR divisions are category II and eight category III. Three of these rifle formations are trained and equipped for mountain operations. Differences between these and other divisions include M-1969 pack mountain guns in place of 122mm weapons and generally lighter scales of equipment.

Turkestan Military District
HQ: Tashkent
   54 MR Div   Termez (?)
   66 (?) MR Div   Samarkand
   84 Gds MR Div 'Karatchev-Orsha-
     Memel'   Kizyl Arvat
   346 MR Div 'Debolzevo'   Kushka (?)
   (?) MR Div   Ashkabad
   ? Arty Div   Bikrava a/o Ashkabad

Several Turkestan MD formations were sent into Afghanistan in 1979-80. Since then two of the divisions originally sent in seem to have been pulled back just inside the district which now has an important back-up mission for the forces across the border. Overall command of operations of Soviet troops in Afghanistan rests with Army-Gen Maximov, the Turkestan district commander. The exact location of units in this area remains uncertain due to frequent redeployments.

Central Asian Military District
HQ: Alma Ata
1st Army   Semipalatinsk
   15 Tk Div (cat I)   Ayaguz

Top:
Moscow MD. This T–34 tank stands on a plinth outside the barracks of the Kantemirov-Shepetova tank division.

Above:
Ural MD. This picture was probably taken in the Ural district in the early 1980s. The AK–74 rifles provide this clue. The outdated T–54/5 tanks are typical of those which make up the bulk of the armoured forces in lower readiness districts. *MoD*

   8 Gds MR Div (cat I) 'Rezhitsa named
     after I. V. Panfilov'   Kurdai
   16 (?) MR Div   Sary Ozek (?)
   80 MR Div   Alma Ata
   165 MR Div   Semipalitinsk
   ? MR Div   Os a/o Karaganda

Also involved in sustaining the Afghan presence this district has two high readiness formations on the Chinese border as well.

Afghanistan
HQ: Kabul
40th Army   Kabul
   105 Gds Air Asslt Div   Bagram
   5 MR Div   Shindand
   201 MR Div   Qonduz
   360 MR Div 'Nevel-Polotsk'   Kabul

American reports on the whereabouts of Soviet forces in Afghanistan have proven consistently contradictory. Whilst Western intelligence agencies gained a good idea of the initial composition of the force from signals intelligence this vital source of information virtually dried up following the laying of land lines by the Russians. Late in 1983

Pentagon sources let it be known that there were three rather than seven motor rifle divisions there. The estimate of manpower (105,000 troops) based on the assumption that there were seven rifle divisions needs to be adjusted downwards and the Americans do not seem to have done this. Around 79,000 Soviet soldiers (including air force, KGB, MVD, and advisory personnel in uniform) remain there, although there are a number of divisions stationed on the Soviet side of the frontier that are able to play a role.

Siberian Military District

HQ: Novosibirsk

23 MR Div 'Elnya-Kiev-Zhitomir'	Biysk
? MR Div	Abakan
? MR Div	Novosibirsk
? MR Div	Tumen

Left:
Central Asian MD. This monument in Alma–Ata commemorates the war feats of the 8th Guards 'Panfilov' Motor Rifle Division. *Tass*

? MR Div	Omsk
? MR Div	Itatke

Of these divisions one is category II and five category III. In common with other districts on the Sino-Soviet border it was strengthened following the frontier clashes of the 1960s.

Transbaikal Military District
HQ: Chita

6 Tk Div	Kyakhta
49 Tk Div	Chita
34 MR Div	Sretensk
9 Gds MR Div 'Borislav-Chinghan'	
	Ulan Ude (?)
? Gds MR Div 'Port Arthur'	Irkutsk (?)
19 Gds MR Div 'Borisov-Rudnensky'	
	Borzia (?)
? Gds MR Div 'Kherson-Breslau-	
Chinghan'	Nizhne pinsk (?)
? MR Div	Dauriya
? MR Div	Borzia
? MR Div	Baklashi

Forces in Mongolia

39th Army	Ulan Bator
5 (?) Gds Tk Div (cat I) 'Stalingrad-Kiev'	
	Choybalsan
91 (?) Gds MR Div (cat I) 'Dukhovshchina-Chinghan'	
	Sayn-Shand
? Tk Div (cat II)	Baran Urt a/o Buigan
? MR Div (cat II)	Sumber Soma

The Transbaikal district was formed largely from the Transbaikal Front, one of those which decimated Japan's Kwangtung Army in 1945. During the early 1970s there was an

Above right:
Armour of the 6th Guards Tank Army crossing the Great Chinghan range in northeastern China in August 1945. A number of formations in the Transbaikal district and Mongolia carry the title Chinghan in honour of this feat of arms. *Novosti*

Right:
Far Eastern MD. BTR–60PBs belonging to the Border Troops of the Pacific Border District. These men bore the brunt of the fighting with the Chinese during the border clashes of the late 1960s and early 1970s. *Novosti*

important expansion of the forces under this HQ, and in 1974 the district received the Order of Lenin, an honour previously held only by the Moscow and Leningrad districts. This HQ in Chita is also believed to control the Soviet garrison in Mongolia, there being a long history of military co-operation between the two countries. In a number of cases the locations given for divisions are somewhat speculative. Three of the rifle divisions are category I, one category II, and four category III.

Far Eastern Military District

HQ: Chabarsovil

5th Army	Ussuriyask
15th Army	Yuzhno-Sakhilinsk
? Corps	Yuzhno-Sakhilinsk
6 Gds Air Asslt Div (cat I) 'Kremenchug-Znamenka'	Belogorsk
? Tk Div	Sebuchar
? Tk Div	Prograncynye
17 Gds MR Div	Barabash
29 MR Div	Kamen-Rybolov
31 MR Div 'Stalingrad'	Belogorsk
73 MR Div	Komsomalska-Amur
79 MR Div	Leonipovo-Sakhilinsk
265 MR Div	Vozhayevka
194 MR Div 'Rezhitsa-Slonim-Luninets'	Khabarovsk
342 MR Div	Yuzhno-Sakhilinsk
88 (?) MR Div 'Krasnodar-Riga-Kharbin'	Lesozavodsk (?)
? MR Div 'Pacific Ocean'	Ussuriyask (?)
? MR Div	Svobodnye
? MR Div	Raychikhimski
? MR Div	Blagovershensk
? MR Div	Dzeingy
? MR Div	Birobidzhan
? MR Div	Lermontovka
? MR Div	Sebuchar
? MR Div	Sergeyeveka
? MR Div	Prograncynye
? MR Div	Babstovo
? MR Div	Smolyaninovo
? Arty Div	Ussuriyask

Around half of these formations are category III. The 5th Army was transferred to the 1st Far Eastern Front in 1945 after campaigning in Europe, and the honours of some of the divisions reflect this. Since the increase in tension on the Chinese border this has become an increasingly important command, second only to GSFG in the combat resources at its disposal.

4. FUELLING THE WAR MACHINE

★

MANPOWER AND SUPPLY

If it is to wage war the Soviet Army requires a constant supply of men and materiel. Of these commodities by far the most important is the quantity and quality of its manpower.

The Soviet Army is largely a conscript force: an estimated 1,400,000 of the Ground Forces' 1,825,000 men are national servicemen. They are drawn from all walks of life and from all of the USSR's many nationalities. The mixing of these ethnic groups with their own cultures and often languages can potentially cause both political and practical problems. It is often claimed in the West that certain nationalities are deliberately excluded from particular units and positions of command, but this view is largely inaccurate. Photographs of combat units taken in Czechoslovakia and Afghanistan which clearly were not posed show a fair distribution of nationalities among the soldiery. It is claimed particularly that the elite units are recruited on a 'Slavs only' basis. The Soviets themselves are sensitive to these allegations and one publication (*Ogonyok*, 1978) claimed recently that there were servicemen from 49 different nationalities in the 76th Guards Air Assault Division.

It is accepted in the Soviet media that education in some remote parts of the country is not of the same standards as that in the towns. The ethnic minorities which by live and large in these more remote areas are therefore at something of an educational disadvantage when they enter the Army. Entrance exams for officer academies are of course in Russian and a poor grasp of the language will result in rejection. The evidence is nevertheless that if they are sufficiently able and determined the minorities can reach the highest positions of command. Army-Gen Tretyak who commands the Far Eastern MD is of Jewish origin. Some claim that these are merely token appointments, but how many black generals are there in the British Army? What we must never forget however is that any minority soldier or politician who seeks advancement in the Soviet system must wholeheartedly embrace the creed of Soviet communism which binds the ruling elite together more closely than any bond of nationality.

There may be a slightly higher than average proportion of ethnic minorities in construction battalions and a lower than average proportion in certain elite units, but it is wrong to say this is the result of any deliberate official policy. Among the soldiers there may be derogatory names for Jews or Kazakhs or bullying of Tartars and Mongols but these manifestations of grass-roots prejudice and ignorance have their parallels in any Western army.

The practical implications of integrating the USSR's nationalities into a single fighting organism are of greater importance. Although during the Great Patriotic War there were a number of 'ethnic' formations such as the Latvian Rifle Division these were phased out in the postwar period. Formations still carry the honorary titles 'Georgia', 'Armenia' and 'Turkestan', a relic of the time when they were raised in those areas, but they are not believed to have an above average number of recruits from these today. It is now the standard practice to evenly mix the nationalities in each unit. Before or during a war category II and III divisions would be topped up with local reservists and might assume a more pronounced ethnic character. The formations sent into Afghanistan in 1979 for example had a higher proportion of central Asian reservists, but after a number of troop rotations a more even mix came about. There can be little doubt however that the policy of mixing recruits can cause elementary problems of communication in infantry sections or tank crews. The USSR is caught between the need to use a single language in its military machine, whilst at the same time guaranteeing the nationalities rights to education and culture in their mother tongues — all 100 of them. Although attempts are made to teach the recruits useful Russian phrases it is apparent that problems do occur.

Since the 1967 Law on Universal Military Service, which shortened the period of conscription from three years to two, programmes for pre-military training have assumed a much greater importance. In schools physical education and some rudimentary military skills are taught as part of the 'Ready for Labour and Defence' programme. Since 1968 there have been military instructors (usually retired officers) in secondary schools and they are responsible for organising rudimentary training (such as orienteering, rifle-shooting and basic tactics), and a military summer camp for those about to join the forces. These military instructors also work in a number of factories, performing the same tasks. More elaborate technical training is given to volunteers at centres of the Voluntary Association for Co-operation with the Army Aviation and Fleet (usually known by its Russian acronym DOSAAF). DOSAAF branches are particularly important in the schooling of drivers, mechanics and radio operators, and a lucky few receive instruction in parachuting and skin diving. DOSAAF clubs — of which there are 350,000 in the USSR — also train civilian mechanics and technicians and rent out their services to local enterprises. Open sources lead one to believe that the standard of pre-military training is somewhat uneven, and until uniform levels are achieved training in many units will have to be organised on the basis of the lowest common denominator.

Pre-military training falls under the auspices of the military district commands, as does the system of processing recruits into the Army. This is done by Military Commissariats (commonly referred to in the USSR as Voenkoms) which are charged to select a particular number of men for service. A central commissariat supervises the overall programme with the actual selection of the conscripts taking place at subordinate offices at the *raion* level which corresponds to a small town or parish. According to Western experts the Voenkoms only need to conscript around half of the young men eligible for

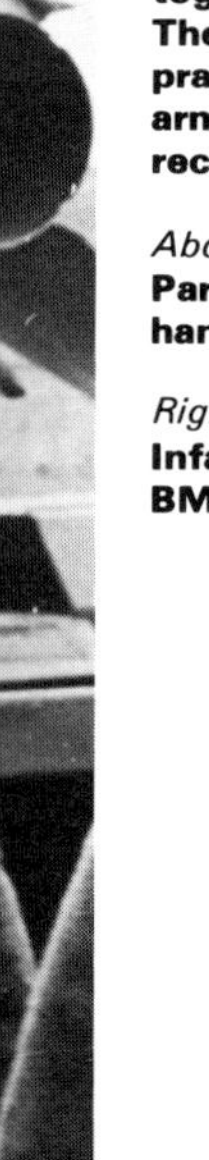

service and exemptions may be granted on educational or medical grounds. Russian emigres have told the author that members of the Voenkoms can be bribed to obtain exemptions from service. Indeed official sources hint that this happens: *Red Star* complained for example of 'citizens being unjustifiably granted a deferment'. Conscripts are given little choice as to where they are sent, although DOSAAF specialist training (eg parachuting) will usually result in a posting to a particular type of unit.

Once conscripted the soldiers undergo four weeks of basic training known as 'The Course of the Young Soldier'. It is only after this that the oath is taken and the conscripts enter the ranks of a proper unit. It is apparently intended to improve the standard of pre-military training to the point where this four-week course is unnecessary. Indeed it is known that some recruits who have received specialist pre-military training are already allowed to take the oath without undergoing 'The Course of the Young Soldier'. Oath-taking ceremonies are often conducted at huge war memorials with the aim of impressing on the young soldiers the patriotic importance of their military service.

There are two call-ups per annum, on 2 May and 1 December, so all training in the units is conducted with these two dates in mind, signalling as they do not only the arrival of the new men but also the exodus of the most experienced conscripts. Training is conducted in six-month cycles, and in each period is aimed at building up unit effectiveness bit by bit, perfecting section drills then platoon ones, etc. Only near the end of the six months will whole battalions exercise together; manoeuvres at regimental and divisional level are rarer and often do not occur in a training year. Army-level exercises involving as they do 50,000 or so troops are rarer still and may not occur in some districts for 10 or more years. Logic dictates that if each conscript serves two years and training is conducted in six-month cycles that each soldier will complete the cycle four times. Attempts are made to train specialists to attain a higher grade each six months; ideally they should become third class specialists after six months and upgrade this each training cycle to become first class or master specialists by the time they leave.

Tactical training involves the repetitive learning of a limited number of drills, eg 'company deploying from line of march'. Rigid adherence to the manuals is essential as the conscripts would in all probability serve in other units in the event of war. Much use is made of training simulators, there being a desire to reduce wear and tear on valuable equipment. It is also reported that track mileage allowances for armoured vehicles are limited to 200km per year. Tank gunners in some garrisons are apparently only given one to two service rounds to fire a year. Although much training is done with sub-calibre tank gun training devices this is no substitute for firing a good number of rounds on a properly constructed range. Although Soviet Army training provides individuals with a sound grasp of their individual tasks by vigorous and repeated lessons on simulators, it seems that large scale exercises in which all members of the 'combined arms team' can combine their skills and learn practical lessons are a rarity. One only has to compare the superb facilities used by many Western armies (for example the British Army range in Canada where whole battle groups fire and manoeuvre under highly realistic conditions) to see that such highly expensive facilities do not come near the top of the Soviet list of spending priorities.

The only Soviet exercises that receive coverage are as spectacular, and as stage-managed, as Hollywood epics. Viktor Suvorov describes the elaborate preparations that were made for the 1967 'Dnieper' exercises: 'Every possible step to ensure nothing went wrong was taken: whole divisions were formed from officers, and river beds where the tanks had to schnorkel were carpeted with steel mesh'. Suvorov comments 'It is impossible to say how much this peep show cost our peace-loving people'. Carefully staged manoeuvres by the Red Army in the 1930s did not prove a very accurate guide to its war fighting capabilities.

The everyday monotony of barrack life rarely changes for the conscripts. Trips outside the barracks are regarded as a privilege and are often granted as a reward for exemplary service. Although soldiers stationed in the European USSR are given passes reasonably frequently (for one only has to see the number of them on the streets of any Soviet city to establish this) those stationed in some of the Warsaw Pact countries are only allowed rare (accompanied) excursions, usually to factories or

Above right:
Accommodation for Russian soldiers has never been luxurious. This dormitory shows the conditions in which the cadets at a prestigious officer academy live. *Novosti*

Below:
In an army where junior NCOs including sergeants are conscripts there is a constant shortage of cadre personnel. *Novosti*

friendship societies. Because their pay is so low ($3\frac{1}{2}$ roubles per month — roughly £3.30) some resort to petty crime, selling Army property to locals, usually to buy drink. Drinking is considered by many Soviet officers to be one of the most serious problems in military life, and one colonel recently wrote to *Red Star* to ask parents not to send money to supplement their sons' meagre pay as they would only spend it on drink.

Junior non-commissioned officers (NCOs) are also usually conscripts who have been selected for cadre training by their Voenkom or have served as soldiers prior to selection. NCO training is conducted largely in the training divisions where six-month courses are run. The newly qualified men are then posted to their respective units. Most will leave the Army when they have completed two years, taking their know-how with them. Because there are very few section leaders or junior tank commanders with any more than two years' experience officers are required to do a great deal of administrative and organisational work themselves. NCOs, in common with other conscripts, are often terrorised and bullied by more senior draftees. According to one former sergeant in the Soviet Army the length of a man's service carries more authority than the stripes on his shoulder. Clearly this mentality undermines NCOs' authority, and thereby damages the workings of the military system at its most basic level. Since 1967 there have been a number of attempts by the military authorities to attract NCOs into a signing on

Left:
Technical training of officer cadets. They spend between three and six years at the academy before being commissioned with the rank of lieutenant. *Novosti*

Below:
Graduating officers from the Higher Command School (named after the RSFSR Supreme Soviet) parade in Red Square. *Novosti*

for regular service. Most significant among these was the reintroduction in 1972 of the *praporschik* (warrant officer) ranks with highly respectable rates of pay and good promotion prospects. Although this and other schemes have been reasonably successful there is still, in the words of Herbert Goldhammer, an expert on Soviet military manpower, 'An unfilled demand for cadre personnel'.

Aspirant officers who have been selected by the Voenkoms are sent to one of the Soviet Union's 140 military schools (analogous to Sandhurst or West Point). Of these 36 belong to the Ground Forces, 24 to the various Special Troops (Engineers, Chemical, Railway, Automotive and Topographic) and five to the Rear Services. The time spent by the cadets will vary from three to six years (the longer course being for specialists) at the end of which they will graduate with the rank of lieutenant and a diploma similar to a university degree. It is estimated that these 140 schools produce 50,000 new officers for the armed forces each year. In 1969 *Red Star* produced statistics about Army lieutenants. A study of prior occupations showed that 37% of them had been to military schools prior to entering the officer academies, 27% had been 'workers', and 20% had been promoted from the ranks. As the requirement for technical specialists has grown so the number of graduate officers has increased from 10% of the total in 1953 to 41% in 1973.

University students receive training as reserve officers from organisations similar to British UOTCs. Soviet law allows for these men to be mobilised for up to three months of the year each year until they are 35. Most graduates however would consider themselves unlucky to be called up more than once or twice. There are certain reserve officers mainly engineers and specialists who do seem to be called on more often than others. They were used in both Czechoslovak and Afghanistan operations. The fact that they had to be mobilised at all for what were essentially limited operations indicates that in any general war they would be indispensable. The quality of these reserve officers who receive only general training at their places of higher education is open to question.

The movement of manpower and supplies to the front lines is the responsibility of the Rear Service. The Soviet concept of the *Tyl* or Rear is an important one embracing all service support within one organisation. Rear services are divided into central (strategic), operational, and troop (tactical) units. A measure of the constantly increasing importance of the *Tyl* corps is that its national chief was recently given the rank of marshal. At the national level and down through each subordinate level of military command there are separate headquarters and staffs for the Chiefs of the Rear, as those responsible for supply are known.

At the national level 90% of supply is carried out by railway, perhaps 5% by road and the remainder by fuel pipeline and air. It is clear then that railways are the key to the strategic supply of the Soviet Army. The rail network (see map) comprises approximately 135,000km of 5ft broad gauge track (and there is an additional 43,000km of narrower gauge trackage). Averaged out for the whole vast country this amounts to 0.62km of line per 100sq km; in the USA for example the figure is 5.8km. There is a relatively high density of railways in the European heartland with lower densities in the peripheral areas. Indeed much of the garrison in the Far East is dependent on the Trans-Siberian Railway which at points passes within 40-50km of the Chinese border. This somewhat unsatisfactory state of affairs is being altered by the construction of the Baikal-Amur Railroad (BAM) which runs farther to the north of the Sino-Soviet frontier. Those on the northern and southern flanks are also dependent on limited railway connections, in places single tracks traversing geographically inhospitable areas. The significance of this is that these routes are easier to monitor before the outbreak of hostilities and to interdict once they have begun.

Within central Europe the Soviets can not complain of any shortage of railroads and they would be used to move second echelon forces forward. Some 42 out of the 44 tank and motor rifle divisions in the Baltic, Carpathian, Byelorussian and Kiev military districts are garrisoned on or very close to railheads. No other method of transport can move heavy equipment to the front as efficiently, and the Manchurian campaign showed how large forces could be transferred between theatres by rail. The movement of one tank army and three combined-arms armies down the Trans-Siberian Railway took $2\frac{1}{2}$ months. The Railway Troops are maintained as a separate service branch and have their own academies and command structure. In war they would be responsible for the security of the railways as well as their upkeep and operation.

The mechanisation of Soviet divisions since the war and the inclusion within the modern formation of so much equipment means that the strategic mobility problem faced by the Soviet Army today is of a completely different order to that of the Great Patriotic War. A motor rifle division today (category I with one BMP and two BTR-60 regiments) has about 220 tanks, 140 BMPs, 250 BTR-60s, 95 scout cars, 54 self-propelled guns, 690 light vans and trucks, 1,600 heavy vans and trucks, 84 towed guns and 36 anti-aircraft vehicles. If we follow the norms set out by Soviet manuals for loading equipment on to trains it is possible to calculate that they need 8-10 hours to carry out this operation at say 10 loading points. We do not know how many wagons could be made available for military use, and thus how many divisions could load at once. There are

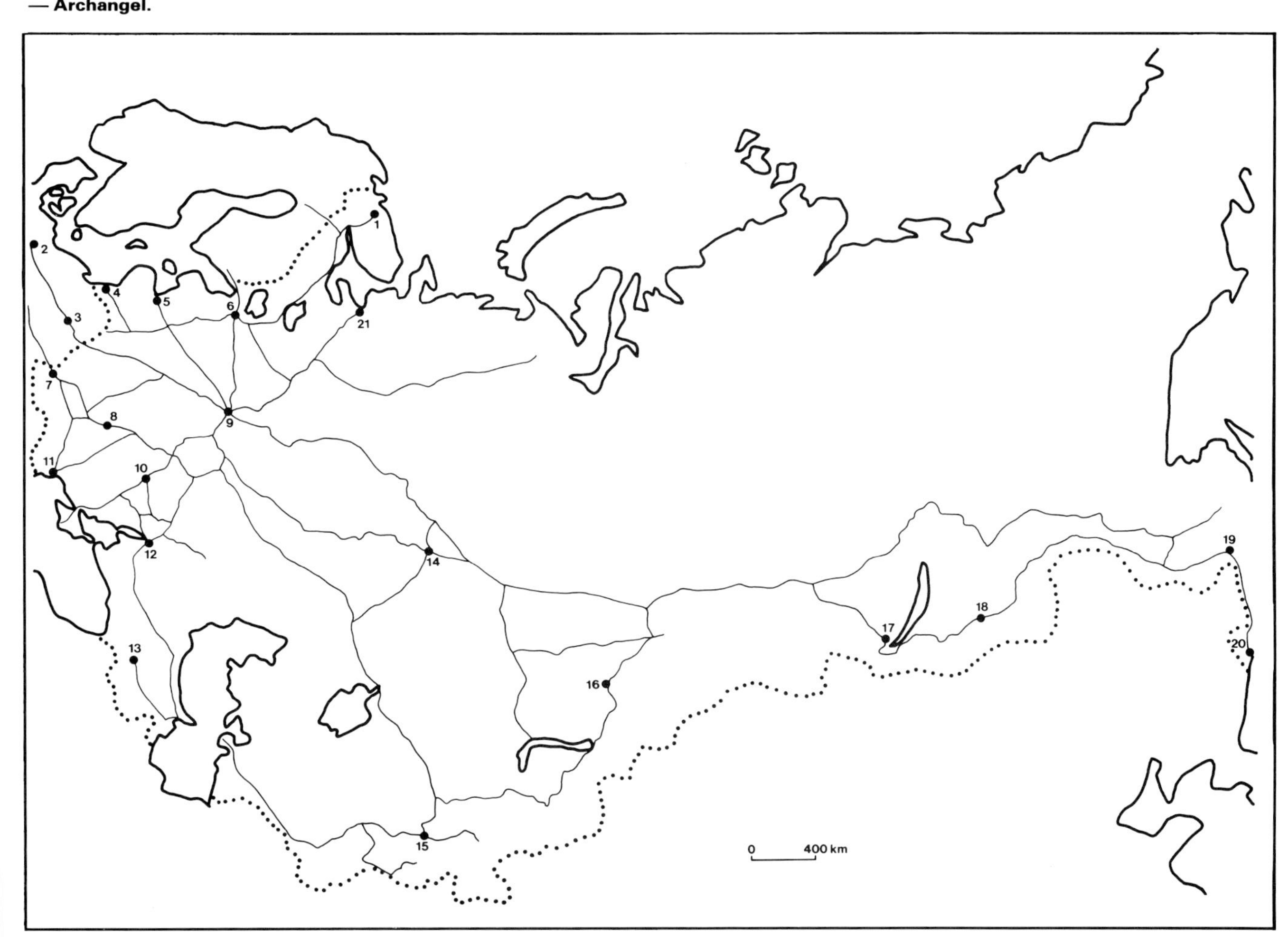

Principal Soviet railway lines

1 — **Murmansk;** *2* — **Berlin;** *3* — **Warsaw;** *4* — **Kaliningrad;** *5* — **Riga;** *6* — **Leningrad;** *7* — **Lvov;** *8* — **Kiev;** *9* — **Moscow;** *10* — **Kharkov;** *11* — **Odessa;** *12* — **Rostov;** *13* — **Tbilisi;** *14* — **Chelyabinsk;** *15* — **Samarkand;** *16* — **Semipalitinsk;** *17* — **Irkutsk;** *18* — **Chita;** *19* — **Khabarovsk;** *20* — **Vladivostock;** *21* — **Archangel.**

only two broad gauge routes across Poland and use of other lines would require reloading of equipment, doubling shipment times. Rail capacity would probably be sufficient to transfer high readiness formations from the western districts to the GDR over a period of say two or three weeks. There are more serious limitations in the Far Eastern theatre where the build-up of forces needed to launch a major attack against the Chinese would take months. In the south too there would be difficulties with only three lines serving the Transcaucasus district. The distance factor combined with limited transport capacity places serious constraints on the Soviet ability to launch surprise actions in the Southern, Far Eastern and Southwest European TVDs.

Because rail installations are fixed they are comparatively easy to monitor, and it is often said that the Soviets' best chance of maintaining surprise against NATO would be to conduct strategic movement by air. The biannual troop rotations in the groups of forces would allow them to surge forward strengths by 15-20% without giving any major signals to NATO. These men could crew the tanks and equipment held in storage in GSFG and could provide a reserve division for each of the group's armies to replace early combat losses. In many sectors though air transport capacities would be strained bringing existing under-strength divisions up to combat readiness rather than transporting new ones into the theatre. Air transport capacity is insufficient to transport the heavily mechanised tank and motor rifle

units in significant numbers. For this reason the Air Assault Forces have since the early 1970s been restructured in the airmobile role, and are now provided with sufficient BMDs to conduct sustained mobile operations. Where Air Assault Forces are unavailable strategic movement by air offers them major possibilities only where equipment has been pre-positioned.

Troops sent from their garrisons to the front line eventually become part of the operational and then the troop or immediate rear. The operational rear extends to between 100 and 150km back from the forward line of troops (FLOT). Supplies in the operational rear are usually controlled by the army *tyl* chiefs who will normally operate base and forward depots. These army level depots are the usual break of bulk points for rail-shipped supplies and terminals for fuel pipelines. In war Rail and Pipeline Troops would extend the track and pipe networks forward into operational areas. Army rear services hold transport for the supply of divisions (and the divisions of their regiments), and in this way

When the 6th Guards 'Kiev-Fastov' division was withdrawn from GSFG in 1979 its T-62s and other vehicles were transported by railway. The Soviet Army depends on this means for 95% of its strategic movement. *Novosti*

Above:
On mobilisation huge quantities of men and materiel would be transported to railheads in East Germany, like this one at Dazu where a Ural-377 command vehicle is being unloaded.

Left:
The scene would be similar in a conflict in the 1980s. : trains with troops and materiels heading for the front lines in 1941. *Novosti*

the army commander is able to channel supplies towards the formations which he feels need or deserve them most. Supplies in the troop rear fall under the aegis of the divisional rear commander, whose control usually extends 30-50km back from the FLOT.

Ammunition is accounted in BKs (*Boevoy Komplekt*, or unit of fire) and fuel in 'fills'. A tank BK for example is the number of rounds normally carried and a fill the amount of fuel needed to replenish the tanks. Different norms for BK and fuel expenditure are established for different types of operation: for example, more ammunition is used in a breakthrough attack, or more fuel in the pursuit. Divisional transport can lift an estimated 3,700 tonnes (motor rifle) or 3,400 tonnes (tank) of supplies, and army organic transport 5,000 tonnes. Frontal resources are sufficient to transport five BKs for all tanks, up to 12 BKs for artillery weapons, and five fuel fills for all vehicles. How long these supplies would last would depend on the intensity of combat, but during the Manchurian campaign logistics for the whole operation amounted to three to five BKs, 10 fuel fills for tanks and 20 for transport. Current fuel transport capability seems a little limited especially in the light of the fact that fuel consumption has risen several fold as a result of the motorisation of units.

The Commandants Service is responsible for traffic control in the rear area. There are so many vehicles in each division and army that it faces a difficult job. A division's vehicles if placed 100m apart would extend on a road for around 176km. If three routes were used then each column would still be 59km long. Obviously these figures are over-simplified, but they should serve to alert the reader as to the scale of the problem that Soviet Army planners would face in war. Without superb staff work and rear control they will find themselves with enormous traffic jams and bottlenecks posing irresistible targets for NATO artillery and aviation. In some areas geography confines all traffic to a few roads slowing the development of operations and the speed of advance. Examples might be the Caucasus mountains or the tundra of the Kola peninsula (bordering Norway) where cross-country movement by normal vehicles is impossible for much of the year.

The ability of the army to keep fighting

Above:
Unlike many Western armies the Soviets have few tank transporters.

Below:
Increasingly, biannual troop rotations are carried out by air. It takes about three weeks for GSFG to complete each troop rotation.

Left:
A fuel terminal in East Germany. New pipe sections stand ready to extend the network in war.

Right:
Supply at its most basic. Troops queue for a meal at the field kitchen. *Novosti*

Below right:
BTR-60s move out of a hide directed by a member of the Commandants Service whose members control movement in the rear area. *via C. F. Foss*

once initial stocks have been expended will depend on the size and accessibility of its war stocks. The length of time that it can sustain conventional combat is also important in determining if and when weapons of mass destruction would be used. In common with many Western armies the Soviets expanded their ammunition stocks substantially after the 1973 Middle East war, when the protagonists used up their bombs and bullets far quicker than they expected. Today the Soviets' total ammunition stockpile is estimated at 10million tonnes, stored at about 70 major and many more minor dumps around the USSR. Pentagon experts estimate that they have sufficient stockpiles to keep their forces in central Europe supplied for 60 to 90 days and those in the Far East for 60 days. There are a number of large armoured vehicle depots storing equipment for low readiness divisions. These are near Novgorod, Kiev, Oster, Kharkov, Moscow, Sverdlovsk, Alma Ata, Tbilisi, Ulan Ude, Khabarovsk and Vladivostock. Most of the hardware in these depots is of World War 2 or early postwar vintage.

Nearly all of their nuclear warheads are stockpiled in the USSR itself, there being very few with the forward-based forces. By contrast NATO stores its warheads near user units, there being 5,000 nuclear devices in West Germany alone. Marshal Ustinov has stressed the need for 'still more rigid control for the assured exclusion of the unsanctioned launch of nuclear weapons from tactical to strategic'. This remarkable statement implies a lack of confidence in even senior officers. The result is that that the Soviet Army's nuclear warheads are stored at clusters of special sites. These complexes of nuclear weapons storage facilities are around Kaliningrad, Klaipeda and Kaunas in the Baltic republics, Nevel in Byelorussia, Lvov, Ivano-Frankovsk, Berdichev, Kharkov and Odessa in the Ukraine, Ulan Ude and Chita in the Transbaikal, Baku in the Caucasus, and around Vladivostock on the Pacific seaboard. The Chita facilities are also associated with the Strategic Rocket Forces as are installations around Novosibirsk and Sverdlovsk. The Navy too stores nuclear weapons on the Kola peninsula, in the Crimea, Vladivostock and Petropavlovsk. The guarding and control of the warheads rests with an element of the KGB's Security Troops reportedly called 'Section K'. In time of crisis the warheads would be despatched to units via nuclear weapons depots at theatre and front levels. The transportation of warheads is routinely listed in Soviet literature on logistics as the number one priority. The involvement of the KGB and storage arrangements show that the Soviets aim to keep the tightest possible political control of nuclear weapons.

Although the production capabilities of the Soviet defence industries are impressive by any standards they are not limitless and it is worth remembering that as late as the mid-1970s some allies were being supplied with the T-34 tank. The assumption that nuclear release would occur within five-seven days of

the outbreak of hostilities has led NATO governments to hold only sufficient war stocks to fight conventionally for 14 days. One can not help but feel that this policy is mistaken, because after all, NATO forces only have to hold out for this period before they will begin to run out of ammunition and sector commanders will only then have nuclear weapons to rely on.

Soviet statistical data shows that tank formations suffered average losses of 30% in the major operations of the Great Patriotic War. The forces of GSFG (ie five armies) might expect to lose 1,800-2,200 tanks in the crucial breakthrough of week one of a future war, and perhaps 3,000 by the week two mark. Significantly this is approximately the number of older tanks held in forward storage in GSFG. Within a week of fighting T-54/5s and T-62s would form around half the strength of even the front line forces. Applied to NSWP contingents these loss rates mean that they would be using large numbers of T-34s and other obsolete vehicles before the end of week two.

Warsaw Pact doctrine favours the withdrawal of units from the front line and their replacement with fresh forces rather than continued 'topping-up' of the original formations with reserves. Given the kind of loss rates that would occur they would have to have forces from the strategic second echelon available to take over the advance in some sectors between the third and fifth days of the offensive.

As we saw earlier Military Doctrine places a great emphasis on actions throughout the enemy depth. The most important single element in the Soviet capability to do this are the Air Assault Forces (VDV). This 73,000-strong corps is organised into eight combat divisions but would normally only be parachute-dropped in battalion or regimental groups. They would sieze important objects such as key bridges, ground of vital importance, nuclear weapons and airfields. In addition to their parachute role they can also be used rapidly to reinforce weak sectors, and for the projection of power beyond the USSR's borders. The VDV form a special reserve under the command of the General Staff and a number would be assigned to TVD headquarters in war. The most important constraint on the use of these VDV divisions is the lack of airlift capability, for in war it is estimated that little more than 20% of VTA capacity could be used for air-drops.

In recent years new tactical units have been developed to exploit the tactical possibilities offered by the helicopter. There are three airmobile brigades (based in the Transcaucaus, Transbaikal and Far Eastern MDs) each consisting of around 1,750 men organised into three rifle battalions and various support units. There are also 10 air assault brigades (one each in Afghanistan, GSFG, Southern Group of Forces, Leningrad, Baltic, Byelorussian, Carpathian, Odessa, Central Asian and Far Eastern MDs) consisting of 2,500 men organised into four rifle battalions (two parachute trained), and support units including an artillery battalion.

The fleet Naval Infantry regiments are equipped for sea landings in battalion and regimental strength. Sea lift capabilities are limited and likely operational targets would all be fairly close to home ports: the Baltic approaches, northern Norway, the Dardanelles and northern Japan. By the standards of the VDV the Naval Infantry is still a small and poorly equipped corps but it would still have an important role to play in any conflict.

The elite behind the lines forces are the Spetznatz or Diversionary Troops. The 1,000-man Spetznatz brigades are assigned very roughly one per front or fleet. These men, who fall under the organisational aegis of the Main Intelligence Directorate (GRU) of the General Staff, would carry out a whole variety of operations ranging from reconnaissance to sabotage, assassination and the

direction of partisan groups. Normally they would operate in small teams, like the British SAS, but some target might necessitate company or even brigade strength operations.

A number of elements have the task of deep penetration reconnaissance. Long Range Reconnaissance Patrols are the most numerous being organic to most divisions and armies. There are also a number of small GRU and KGB intelligence gathering teams. Each fleet has a Naval Infantry Commando platoon which would be used rather like the British Special Boat Section.

The Soviets' way of war involves attacks throughout the enemy's depth, and they in turn expect the same to be done to them. Western naval supremacy means that its amphibious forces might well be employed for landings perhaps in the northern USSR or on the Pacific seaboard, and these might be up to divisional strength. Airborne forces might also be used to attack rear lines: the US 82nd Airborne Division and West German 1st Airborne Division are the two most important Western forces. A NATO strategy that would prove more difficult to counter would be the use of diversionary troops in small numbers. These include the British SAS and US Special Forces, and many would operate in the stay-behind role remaining in hideouts until Soviet forces had passed over, or might be inserted even deeper into the rear. Missions would include

The Strategic Air Assault Operation

In peacetime as well as war the Air Assault Forces are the best means of securing strategic objectives far from Soviet frontiers.

Far top left:
H−8 Special Forces and Air Assault Forces pathfinders land deep in the enemy rear and prepare drop zones. *Novosti*

Above left:
H−3. Paratroops board an Antonov transport. *Novosti*

Left:
H−3. Il−76s pick up their passengers at another air head.

Far bottom left:
H−Hour. A 120mm mortar lands on its air dropping pallet. *Novosti*

Below left:
H−Hour. A BMD crew prepares its vehicle for combat after air dropping on its special pallet. *via C. F. Foss*

Right:
H+5. The air-dropped regiment seizes an airhead and is reinforced rapidly by air. *Novosti*

Below:
H+24. The air-landed task force moves towards its final objective. New equipment introduced since the 1960s, such as these PVD−20 inflatable rafts and BMDs, has given the VDV the ability to mount independent mobile operations in the strategic rear. *Novosti*

sabotage, reconnaissance, attacks on headquarters, airfields, communications installations and railways, and the organising of partisan activities. NATO special forces might well adopt Warsaw Pact weapons and uniforms in order to carry out their missions.

In Soviet field force HQs rear area security is the responsibility of the Chief of the Rear. Great Patriotic War rear security operations give us a good idea how they would be conducted today. Each army was assigned a regiment of NKVD (modern equivalents are MVD Internal or KGB Border Troops) and after 1944 each front was assigned a further NKVD division as well; by that year the number of troops devoted to rear security had reached 80,000. Between August and September 1944 the 37th Border Regiment serving the 52nd Army killed 1,700 and captured 720 enemy officers and men. Army rear zones were designated 'forward security zones' and everything behind this came under frontal jurisdiction. Forward zones were divided into sectors under the control of battalions which were further split into regions controlled by companies.

Within these regions security forces will conduct patrols and vehicle check-points, round up suspects, deal with prisoners of war and set up liaison points between army rear areas. The responsibility for the forward zone would fall to elements of the Main Directorate of Border Troops (GUPV). The GUPV has around 300,000 men grouped into nine frontier districts. Detachments (as regimental-sized units are known) have 1,000-1,500 men and are the largest field units of the Border Troops. About 60% of total GUPV strength is concentrated on the Chinese border where there have been a number of incidents over the last 15 years.

The Ministry of the Interior (MVD) Internal Troops number around 200,000 and are grouped into regiments and divisions similar to those of the Army in equipment and organisation (although with less tank support and more antiquated kit). These forces are deployed throughout the USSR as a back-up to the Militsia (police). MVD provincial HQs in the Ukraine, Baltic provinces, Byelorussia and the Caucasus each control Internal Troops to divisional strength. There is an MVD division in Moscow, the 1st Felix Dzerzhinski Motor Rifle Division of Special

Below:
Men of the MVD Internal Troops march in a western Russian town.

Above right:
Border Troops under training: in war they could be used to secure the rear area. *Tass*

Designation, which has an important role in securing governmental installations. MVD regiments and divisions in the western USSR might be earmarked to move forward into eastern Europe in war under the control of frontal HQs. MVD tasks would include route and convey security as well as the administration of prisoner-of-war camps.

The elite paramilitary organisation is that of the KGB State Security Troops controlled by the 9th Directorate. They number perhaps 25,000 men organised into regiments and battalions, and many are stationed in Moscow where they are responsible for the security of the leadership and the guarding of key Party and government buildings. They are charged with the control of nuclear warheads. Elements from the border, MVD Internal and State Security Troops have been identified in Afghanistan performing security missions.

Each of the NSWP countries possesses its own internal forces and these would play an important role in securing the Pact rear in the early stages of a conflict as the movement of Soviet internal forces would initially at least be a low priority. The GDR in particular has impressive numbers of paramilitary troops. Border Guard and Alert Police battalions would be placed under Soviet commanders in war to secure the forward zone and Workers Militia would protect static installations.

Above left:
These men of the KGB's 9th Directorate are part of the Soviet leadership's praetorian guard. They protect key installations, act as bodyguards for leaders and control nuclear warheads.

Below:
East Germany's border guards form part of the large NSWP internal security force. *ADN*

5. TOOLS FOR THE JOB

★

DEFENCE INDUSTRIES AND ARMAMENT

There can be no doubt that the war industries of the USSR are in production of equipment for the ground forces the greatest in the world. It is sometimes said that in the West that the only element of the Soviet economy that works really well is that which produces weapons. It is the proud claim of Army-Gen V. Shabanov, Deputy Minister of Defence for Armaments, that 'The Soviet Army and Navy today possess everything necessary for the reliable defence of the gains of socialism, for the decisive defeat of any aggressor'. We shall examine both the system by which the weapons are produced and the hardware itself.

Requests for new equipment are formulated in the main staffs of the five services (eg Ground Forces) on the basis of information provided by service armaments directorates, staffs, scientific-technical committees and field commanders. The General Staff also has a role in requesting new weapons and members apparently look mainly at new technologies rather than existing ones. These requests are examined at the highest level by the Council of Defence sitting with additional technical experts. Discussions take place at this stage in the Defence Industry and Machine Construction Department of the Central Committee Secretariat and it determines the availability of resources for the project. From an early point in the development design teams will be working on concepts and building prototypes. Some of these design bureaus, usually named after their founding chief engineer (many of whom have since died), have a virtual monopoly on the development of particular systems, for example the F. F. Petrov artillery design team and the Mil helicopter bureau. Once the politico-military authorities have decided that a particular system is suitable and 'affordable' the Military-Industrial Commission of the Council of Ministers will allocate the work to specific ministries and factories. The State Planning Commission (GOSPLAN) will then organise the plant, labour and raw materials necessary to deliver the finished product.

The system seems to work well with the

Right:
An 'Aist' class assault hovercraft under construction in Leningrad. The introduction of these vessels has greatly enhanced the fighting power of the Naval Infantry.

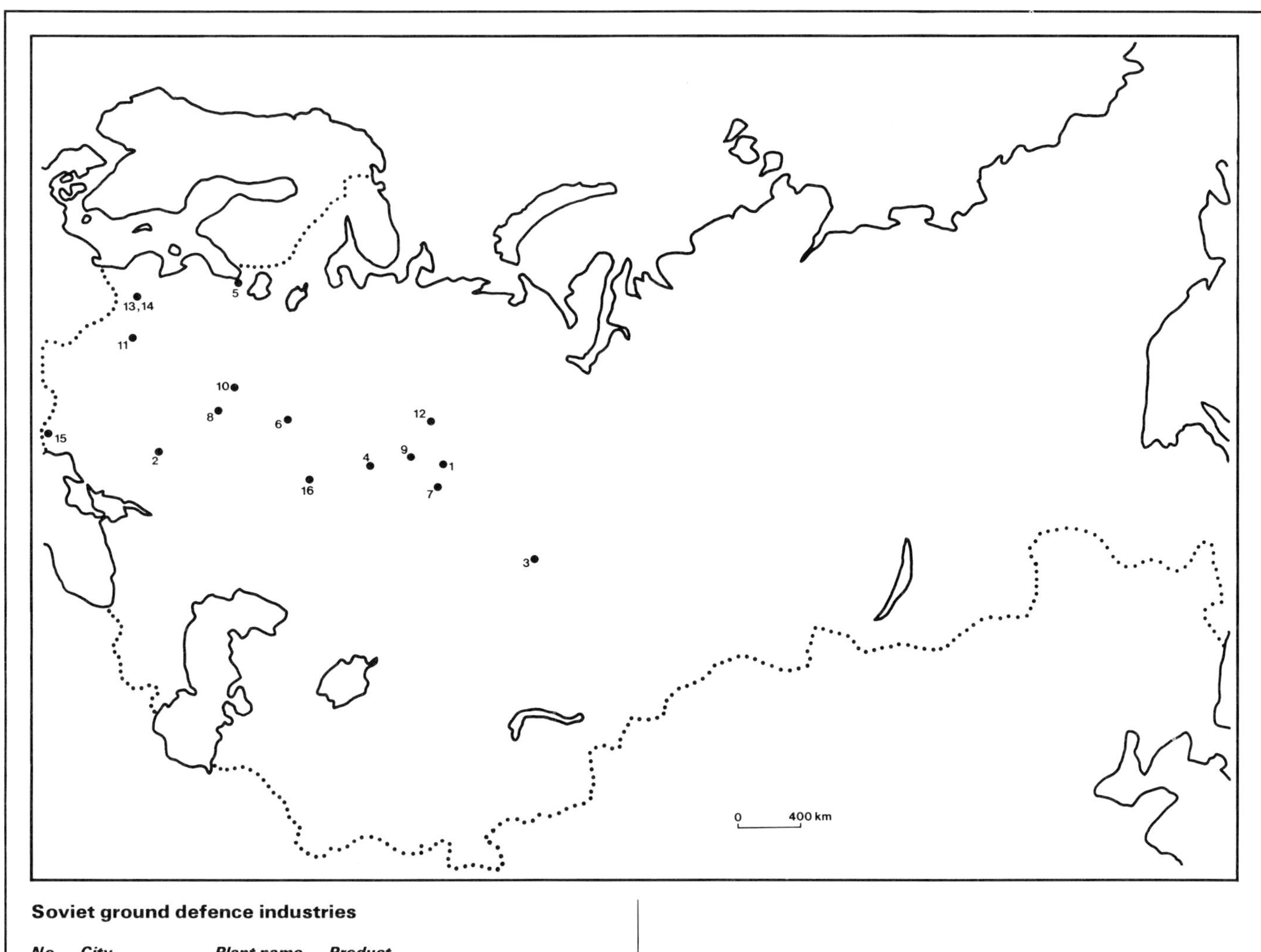

Soviet ground defence industries

No	City	Plant name	Product
1	Nizhniy Tagil	No 183	T-74 and T-72 tanks (formerly T-62 and T-55)
2	Kharkov	Malyshev No 75	T-74 (formerly T-64 and T-62)
3	Omsk	No 174	2S1 and 2S3 and probably T-72
4	Izhevsk	?	BMP and possibly BMD
5	Leningrad	Kirov	Probably ZSU-23, possibly MT-LB (formerly PT-76)
6	Gorkii	Molotov GAZ	BTR-70, BRDM-2, GAZ trucks and jeeps (formerly BTR-60)
7	Sverdlovsk	No 9	D-30 gun-howitzer
8	Tula	No 535	Towed guns
9	Perm	No 172	Towed guns
10	Moscow	Likachev ZIL	TELs for 'Frog-7', 'Frog-9', SA-8 and ZIL range of trucks
11	Minsk	MAZ	TELs for 'Scud-B' and 'Scaleboard', MAZ range of trucks
12	Nabarezhe-nye Chelny	KAMAZ	Kamaz series of trucks
13	Vilnus	Telekom-ponent	Radars
14	Vilnus	No 555	Radios
15	Kishinev	Luch	Computers and other electronics
16	Ulyanovsk	VM	Computers and other electronics

Note: This list includes only the major factories involved in production of equipment for the Ground Forces, many more are assigned to the production of sub-components and minor items.

new technology being assimilated rapidly. During the Brezhnev era the Soviet Army enjoyed a healthy flow of high quality systems. This was due in part to the fact that the Minister of Defence, Marshal Ustinov, had been head of the defence industries for 20 years. It was also due to the fact that the Soviet Army is able to resist the challenge for resources by other sectors of the economy by cloaking its requests for hardware in secrecy.

The map and the key show the principal centres of weapons production in the USSR. Tank production is concentrated at three locations and is currently running at about 2,500 vehicles a year. During the war tank production reached a peak of 29,000 in 1944. It is interesting to note that there has been a fall in production of tanks since 1970. Production at the massive Nizhniy plant has not exceeded 2,500 units per annum in the last 20 years. Only Nizhniy Tagil can produce tanks fast enough to modernise significantly the Soviet tank fleet. Vehicles (such as T-62 and T-64) produced at Kharkov and Omsk can be little more than stop-gap measures for the high readiness divisions as these plants cannot produce tanks fast enough to replace a significant element of the

tank force before they themselves are out of date. The real modernisation of the Soviet tank fleet from T-34 to T-54 and from T-54 to T-72 requires at least 15 years of production at Nizhniy Tagil. At Kharkov the peacetime ceiling is around 1,000 vehicles and it is below this at Omsk. Battle tank manufacturing at Omsk has been much reduced since 1980-81. This plant is probably responsible for production of 2S1 and 2S3 self-propelled guns. For this reason post-1970 production of tanks has not exceeded the 1979-80 total of 3,100 units.

One of the greatest errors committed in Western analyses of Soviet land power is to assume that the total number of weapons corresponds to the number that each division should have multiplied by the total of divisions. But it is not safe to assume that every Soviet division has its full war stocks of equipment: our calculations should be based on the actual production of these items. Viktor Suvorov states that a division in the Kiev MD in which he served only had 40 armoured personnel carriers when it should in fact have had 240. During the 1979 Afghanistan action the 360th Motor Rifle Division arrived in Kabul with early World War 2 vintage artillery.

Soviet production of the T-54/5 lasted from 1949 to 1979 and was centred at Nizhniy Tagil. Between 1949 and 1969 production averaged 2,000 per annum, and between 1969 and 1979 (roughly speaking) 500 per annum, so the total production was around 45,000. About 20,000 have been exported by the Russians which leaves them with a maximum of 25,000. T-62 production at the Malyshev No 75 Plant in Kharkov began in 1961 (and was subsequently extended on a limited basis to Nizhniy Tagil) and probably ended in 1970. Average annual production from these plants was about 1,500, so the total was around 13,500. It is evident that T-62 was not a success and the Soviets have taken every opportunity to sell it abroad, and exports total 5,800 units. This leaves their army with 7,500 of them. Experimental production of the T-64 began as early as 1967 with only a few units being turned out at first. Peak production of 1,000 per annum was reached in the mid-1970s and the total of 5,000-6,000 is more than is often suspected. T-72 major deliveries began in 1974 and by the beginning of 1984 deliveries of T-72 and T-80 (also called T-74) total approximately 12,000 (exports to date of 2,000 leaving the Russians with 10,000).

Total production of postwar main battle tanks not exported, as at 1 January 1984, can therefore be broken down as follows:

T-72/T-80:	10,000 (20%)
T-64:	5,500 (11%)
T-62:	7,500 (15%)
T-54/5:	25,000 (50%)
T-10:	2,000 (4%)

The total of 50,000 therefore represents the highest possible figure for the Soviet tank fleet, excluding World War 2 models. In

Weapons and Tactics of the Soviet Army
David Isby estimates that Soviet divisions require 45,000 tanks, and that there are a further 3,000 units in forward storage in GSFG, so the two figures correspond quite closely. Things are not this simple, for up to this point we have assumed that all vehicles (in particular T-54/5s) which were produced and not exported, some of which are over 30 years old, are still serviceable, and clearly this is not the case. Exactly how many have been destroyed or simply worn out to the point where the only useful function they can play is as range targets is impossible to say, but may amount to 10-20% of the total.

Assembly of self-propelled guns is probably centered at Omsk and production of both models (2S1 and 2S3) can be estimated at an average of 250 units per annum 1973-78 and 450 units 1978-83. Of the 3,500 produced so far perhaps 800 have been exported, leaving 2,700. This would be enough to equip 50 divisions (on the basis of two 2S1 battalions and one of 2S3s per division), although the actual number of self-propelled gun battalions in each formation tends to vary. Almost all of these weapons seem to have gone to the groups of forces and selected high readiness formations in the Western MDs.

Production of the wheeled BTR-60 and BTR-70 model armoured personnel carriers is at the enormous Gorkiy Automobilova Zavod (GAZ) factory. This plant also produces BRDM series scout cars. It is believed that BMPs are manufactured at Izhevsk, around 11,000 being produced (and 2,000 exported) between 1967 and 1978, indicating an average annual production rate of 1,000. Introduction of the BMP began in 1967 and at first it replaced BTR-50s in tank formations. Later a number of motor rifle divisions received sufficient to equip one regiment, although the majority use the wheeled BTR-60 and BTR-70 types. Older BTR-50 and BTR-152 models will account for around 30% of the APC fleet and are concentrated in the lower readiness units. BMD (Airborne Combat Vehicle) manufacture may also be at Izhevsk and if reports that all three combat regiments of the eight combat ready airborne divisions are equipped with them are accurate a total of about 2,800 have been produced.

The main manufacturers of trucks and light vehicles for the Soviet Army are ZIL in

Moscow and GAZ. It is not known what the annual production of military trucks is, although the Soviets claim a figure of half a million trucks and buses for the entire economy. The experience of Czechoslovakia and Afghanistan is that there is a shortage of such vehicles, and preparation for major operations would involve the commandeering of a great deal of motor transport from civilian enterprises.

If we combine what we know about production with unit readiness and deployment data we can draw a number of conclusions. Postwar battle tank production has been just enough to meet Soviet and export needs. Many Russian emigres have however referred to the practice of keeping the newest equipment in storage whilst training on the older models. This practice is thought to occur in the groups of forces and western MDs. If it is at all widespread then we can only conclude that there are insufficient tanks (T-54 and newer) to equip the lower readiness formations. Even in the early 1980s there are Soviet Army divisions that would have to go to war in T-34/85, T-44, JSIII and T-10 tanks. In other units half of the tanks are still T-54/5s built at the same time as British Centurions. These T-54/5s are concentrated in the reserve, southern and eastern districts, where older APCs and artillery also predominate. At current rates of production

it will be at least 1987-88 before the T-64, T-72 and T-80 (T-74) combined account for over half of the Soviet inventory. By this date deliveries of Western tanks such as the M1 Abrams, Leopard 2 and Challenger will also be advanced. Production of the BMP which currently accounts for just over a third of the APC fleet needs to continue (at current rates) until 1988-89 to reach the 50% of total mark.

If we examine the Non-Soviet Warsaw Pact states the equipment situation is (for them) less healthy. In these states at the beginning of 1984 a good 90% of the tank fleets consists of T-54/5 models. Many of these have been produced at plants in Poland and Czechoslovakia. BMPs are in short supply accounting for 15-20% of APC fleets. Figures for Warsaw Pact missile production are impossible to find at the unclassified level so we can only guess at holdings of these. According to David Isby's figures, by 1978 there were enough SA-4 systems (1,077) to equip 38 army and front level air defence brigades. SA-6s existed only in sufficient numbers to equip 33 divisional anti-aircraft regiments. Even if production since then, and the introduction of the new SA-8 has been sufficient to double this figure, it is still evident that over 60% of Soviet divisional anti-aircraft regiments are equipped with S-60 57mm guns.

There can be little doubt that Soviet-

Above:
**Czech T-55s on exercise. This
tank has formed the backbone of
the Pact's fleet since the 1960s.**
ADN

Left:
**A US Army T-62 of the
Opposition Force which simulates
Soviet tactics for NATO troops.**
via C. F. Foss

designed tanks of the Great Patriotic War, and in particular the T-34, were among the finest fielded by any army. T-34/85s were also used with impressive results in the Korean War of 1950-53. Soviet tank constructors were soon looking for ways to improve on the design, and in 1944 the T-44 appeared. It had a more compact hull made possible by mounting the engine transversely and eliminating the hull gunner from the crew. It was produced in limited numbers and may still be found in some category III formations. It was superseded by the T-54, another logical evolution which made use of the T-44's hull but with a turret redesigned to take the D-10 100mm gun.

Series production of T-54 began in 1949 and only ended in the USSR in 1979. At the time of its introduction it was a remarkable achievement combining impressive firepower with tried and tested automotive assemblies. It became the medium tank of the Soviet Army, the worthy successor of the T-34, and saw action around the world. Early models had shot traps (overhangs) at both the front and rear of the turret, but these were soon eliminated giving rise to the distincitve rounded turret. Continuous production improvements resulted in the T-55 with infra-red fighting aids and greater ammunition storage (43 rounds versus 34 in the T-54).

Its light weight and simplicity have resulted in exports to nearly 40 countries around the world. On the modern battlefield this tank is outdated. The 100mm gun and stadiametric sights offer first round hit probabilities against exposed stationary tanks at 1,000m of only 50% with armour piercing (AP) and 43% with High Explosive Anti-Tank (HEAT) ammunition. These tanks were decimated by the superb Israeli tank gunners with their Western tanks in the 1967 and 1973 wars.

The T-62 marks the final evolutionary exploitation of the original T-34 design. It packs a big punch with its 115mm smooth bore gun, and has a flatter turret. Production at the smaller plants was short-lived, ending around 1970. By this time the Soviets had realised that a quantum leap, rather than further evolution, in technology would be necessary to match Western advances in firepower and protection. The T-62 has a 50% chance of a first round hit against a stationary tank at 1,500m (with a BR-5 HVAPFSDS round). By comparison the British Chieftain firing APDS with the aid of a laser range-finder (but not fire control computer) has an 85% chance of hitting the same target. The T-62 is an uninspired design in which the crew discomfort and ammunition storage problems of the T-55 were exacerbated. It is interesting to note that even at the height of its production (1966-67) T-62 output did not exceed that of T-55 which in fact continued until 10 years after T-62 production was halted. During the 1973 Middle Eastern war 'elite' Syrian and Egyptian units with T-62s were mauled by Israeli battalions using modified Centurions and Shermans.

As early as 1967 the Soviet Army, well aware of the T-62's limitations, was field-testing a daring new battle tank design: T-64. The boldest innovation was the use of an autoloader for the armament making it the first modern battle tank to use a crew of only three. Its 125mm smooth bore gun uses a laser range-finder, and it was designed with better mobility to put it on a par with the BMP. Mobility improvements included the dropping of the Christie-style suspension system and adoption of a new Western-style torsion bar system with small road wheels and track return rollers to achieve higher cross-country speeds. Inevitably a system which embraced so many new technologies was bound to suffer development problems.

Because of these the Soviets were not prepared to produce T-64 as a T-55 replacement, or to export it to their allies abroad who were clamouring for a vehicle that could match the latest Western tanks. And so when T-55 production at Nizhniy Tagil began to wind down from 1970 they chose to build a tank that would embody T-64's positive characteristics whilst abandoning its less reliable ones: the result was the T-72.

The principal difference between T-72 and T-64 is that the latter used a new

Main Battle Tank Characteristics

	T-72	T-64	T-62	T-55	T-54
Dimensions					
Length w/o gun (m)	6.90	6.40	6.63	6.20	6.20
Length gun fwd (m)	9.20	9.10	9.33	9.0	9.0
Width (m)	3.60	3.40	3.30	3.27	3.27
Height (m)	2.30	2.30	2.40	2.35	2.40
Crew	3	3	4	4	4
Firepower					
Main armament	125mm	125mm	115mm	100mm	100mm
Rds carried for main gun	40	40	40	43	34
Elevation	−5°/+18°	−5°/+18°	−5°/+18°	−5°/+18°	−4°/+17°
Effective range, HVAPFSDS rd (m)	2,000	2,000	1,600	1,000	1,000
Effective range, HEAT rd (m)	1,500	1,500	1,200	800	800
Muzzle velocity, HVAPFSDS (m/sec)	1,615	1,615	1,615	1,000	1,000
Muzzle velocity, HEAT (m/sec)	1,000	1,000	900	900	900
Rate of fire (theoretical/actual)	6/4	6/4	7/4	7/5	7/5
Co-axial MG	7.62mm	7.62mm	7.62mm	7.62mm	7.62mm
AA MG	12.7mm	12.7mm	(1)	(2)	12.7mm
Mobility					
Weight (tonne)	41	38	37.5	36	36
Ground pressure (kg/cm)	0.79	0.72	0.75	0.81	0.81
Vertical step (m)	0.80	0.80	0.80	0.80	0.80
Max trench (m)	2.70	2.70	2.80	2.70	2.70
Engine	V-12	5-cyl	V-12	V-12	V-12
Output (hp)	780	750	580	580	520
Power/weight (hp/tonne)	19:1	20:1	19:1	16:1	14:1
Internal fuel (litre)	1,000	1,000	960	960	800
Range (internal fuel only, km)	450	450	450	500	400
Max road speed	60	70	50	50	50
Protection					
Max hull armour (mm)	?	?	102	99	99
Max turret armour (mm)	?	?	242	203	203
Full CBR system	Yes	Yes	No	No	No

Left:
A column of T-64s on the march. This vehicle used so many new technologies that it suffered many development problems.
Novosti

horizontally-opposed five-cylinder engine, whereas the T-72 returned to using an uprated version of the classic V12. When it was introduced the T-72, like the T-54 when it entered service, was decidedly superior to the models that made up the mainstay of the Western forces (eg Leopard 1 and M60A1). It is a paradox of the Soviets' tank development that the number of tanks possessed is so large that modernisation of the significant part of them (50% or over) can only be achieved in 15 years of production by their biggest plant. Just as the T54/5 lost its edge half-way through its production run so T-72 is losing its superiority to the Leopard 2, M1 and Challenger. All of these vehicles possess protection (in the shape of Chobham armour) and firepower (fire control computers) a generation ahead of T-72. American claims that T-72 has composite or Chobham armour can be treated with scepticism. Special alloys are thought to be used on the glacis plate, but a quick look at T-72 shows that it doesn't have any of the

obvious physical characteristics of a Chobham tank. The Israelis were able to knock out T-72s in Lebanon's Bekaa Valley in 1982 with their 105mm guns. According to the commander whose men encountered them in Lebanon, 'the T-72s burn just like any other tank'. T-80 (T-74) is simply an updated T-72 bearing the same relationship to it as the T-55 bore to the T-54. Many Western experts predict the appearance of a new tank that will have Chobham armour and possibly the designation T-85. If past production patterns are repeated this will be manufactured in limited numbers at Kharkov.

Although the Great Patriotic War provided in the T-34 the starting point for subsequent tank development this was not the case with APCs. Early models such as the BTR-40 and BTR-152 were simply armoured trucks based on the GAZ-63 and Zil-151/7 chassis respectively. Both vehicles were open topped (except for later versions) and unsophisticated, but played an important role in the motorisation of the Soviet infantry; indeed some still serve in cadre formations. The next, and most important, wheeled APC to be fielded was the BTR-60. It was this machine which allowed the Soviets to complete the motorisation of their foot soldiers in 1963. Early models were open topped but fairly soon the PK variant appeared with an armoured roof and then the PB which has the same 14.5mm machine gun turret as the BRDM-2. Today the BTR-60PB is the most numerous APC in the Soviet Army and has seen action in the Middle East, Ethiopia and Afghanistan.

BTR-60 is nevertheless a vehicle with many faults. It uses two six-cylinder petrol engines slaved together, an unnecessarily complex arrangement resulting in many maintenance problems. The Polish OT-64 vehicle which was produced in preference to buying the BTR-60 has a single diesel engine. The armour is thin and the infanteers must dismount by climbing out of exposed roof and side hatches; within the Soviet Army it is apparently nicknamed 'the coffin'. Although it has a hydrojet to propel it through the water it has difficulty climbing anything but the shallowest river bank or beach.

The tracked BTR-50, derived from the PT-76, appeared in 1954 and experienced fewer problems. It was given to tank formations in eastern Europe and the USSR and some still remain in service as command and engineer variants even in high readiness units. Replacement of BTR-50 with a new vehicle, the BMP-1 (Bronevaya Maschina Pekhoty or Infantry Combat Vehicle), began in 1967. The BMP was a bold design, well ahead of its time. It mounts a 73mm gun and 'Sagger' ATGM allowing it to give fire support to the infantry and take on enemy tanks if the situation calls for it. Other important features are thicker armour and an auto-loader for the gun. The infantry section can fire from inside the vehicle and exit in cover from the rear. The vehicle was such a departure from previous practice that a lively debate began in the Soviet military press as to how the vehicle should be used. The BMP saw combat in the 1973 war where doubts were raised about the performance of the 73mm low pressure gun which was said to be inaccurate.

1981 saw the appearance of the BMP-2 which was immediately fielded in Afghanistan. It has a larger two-man turret which mounts a high velocity 30mm cannon and an AT-5 'Spandrel' ATGM. Because the turret is larger the passenger compartment can only carry five or six men. Now there will have to be another rethink of platoon organisations and tactics.

Throughout the 1950s and early 1960s the standard divisional artillery pieces were the M-1938 (M-30) 122mm howitzer, M-74 122mm gun and D-1 152mm howitzer. The M-1938 and D-1 were both wartime models that were produced in enormous quantities. The M-1938 has a limited range (11.8km) but is still found in many category III divisions. It was replaced in many units by the D-30 quick firing 122mm howitzer. This fine weapon has a semi-automatic sliding breach block enabling burst fire of up to eight rounds per minute. The divisional heavy weapons were replaced by the large D-20 152mm gun-howitzer which has a big punch, firing 43kg of high explosive to a distance of 18.5km. This weapon also serves in artillery brigades along with the M-1946 130mm gun. The M-1946 has a long and distinguished record being used to great effect in Vietnam and the Middle East. The Israelis gained such respect for them that they pressed all of the M-1946s they had captured into service and begun producing rounds for them. It is ideally suited to counter-battery work.

Heavy regiments of artillery divisions are equipped with S-23 180mm nuclear-capable guns. These are being replaced in GSFG by a new 203mm gun. Since the early 1970s self-propelled guns derived from the D-30 and

D-20 have entered service. The 122mm weapon is mounted on a vehicle which has much in common with the MT-LB, and the 152mm on one derived from the SA-4 Transporter Erector Launcher (TEL). These weapons have been introduced because the towed guns were not considered mobile enough to keep up with the rapidly advancing armoured formations. In 1982 Western experts identified the 2S5 with a newly designed 152mm weapon, and apparently nuclear capable. This is mounted on a vehicle derived from the SA-4 TEL, but without the enclosed turret of the 2S3. Another trend has been the introduction of a number of command vehicles. The ACRV-2 is now used by forward observers, battery and battalion commanders and carries radio gear, range finding apparatus and perhaps in the near future artillery computers. The BMP-SON is a modified BMP with a large turret mounting a 'Small Fred' artillery locating radar set well to the rear of its hull. It has a range of 39km and would be deployed with units assigned for counter-battery missions.

Divisional anti-tank battalions are often equipped with T-12 100mm anti-tank guns. This smooth bore weapon is effective to 1,500m with armour piercing ammunition, and is particularly useful in defence. The Soviets have continued faith in anti-tank guns and a new 125mm weapon called Rapira 3 may replace the T-12s in due course. Other anti-tank units are armed with

AT-3 'Sagger' and AT-5 'Spandrel' systems mounted on BRDM-2 vehicles. The 'Sagger' proved successful in the 1973 Yom Kippur War but is now somewhat outdated. The AT-4 'Spigot' closely resembles the Western Milan and has been issued to high readiness units.

BM-21 remains the standard multiple rocket launcher (MRL), firing 40 122mm rockets to a distance of 20km. This descendant of the wartime Katyushas can put down very heavy fires suitable for counter-battery work and the laying down of smoke and chemicals. The BM-21 has been in service for 20 years and has fought around the world. It has been replaced in a number of GSFG units by the BM-27, a new 16-barrel 220mm MRL mounted on a chassis derived from the Zil-135 'Frog-7' launch vehicle.

Since the early 1960s Soviet divisions and armies have been equipped with battlefield nuclear missiles. The 'Frog-3' weapon has a 35km range and uses a TEL based on the PT-76, and it is still in cadre and some NSWP divisions. 'Frog-7' rockets on Zil-135 TELs equip the majority of Soviet divisional 'Frog' battalions. 'Frog-7' has a range of 70km and has been in service since 1965. It is now being replaced in high readiness units by the SS-21, or 'Frog-9', which uses a TEL derived from the Zil-167 SA-8 vehicle. These

Above left:
Early BTR-60s were open-topped like this one of the Naval Infantry. *Novosti*

Left:
BMP: heavily armed, mobile and well protected.

Above:
This BMP/BMD turret shows how cramped the gunner's station is. Behind it is an ASU-57 air assault vehicle no longer in front-line use.

Light AFV Characteristics

	BMP-2	BMP-1	BMD	BTR-60BP	BRDM-2	MT-LB
Dimensions						
Length (m)	6.74	6.74	5.41	7.22	5.70	6.45
Width (m)	2.94	2.94	2.55	2.82	2.35	2.85
Height (m)	2.30	2.15	1.77	2.31	2.31	1.87
Crew/passengers	3/7	3/8	3/5	3/8	2/4	2/10
Firepower						
Main gun	30mm	73mm	73mm	14.5mm	14.5mm	7.62mm
Main gun effective range	800	800	800	1,500	1,500	1,000
ATGW	AT-5	AT-3	AT-3	—	—	—
Co-axial	7.62mm	7.62mm	7.62mm	7.62mm	7.62mm	—
Mobility						
Weight (tonne)	14	13.5	8	10.2	7	11.9
Ground pressure (kg/sqcm)	0.60	0.57	0.61	n/a	n/a	0.46
Vertical step (m)	0.80	0.80	0.80	0.40	0.40	0.70
Max trench (m)	2.00	2.00	1.60	2.00	1.60	2.70
Engine type	V-6	V-6	V-6	2 6	V-8	V-8
Petrol/Diesel	D	D	D	P	P	D
Engine output (hp)	290	290	290	180	140	290
Fuel (litre)	460	460	300	290	290	450
Road range (km)	500	500	320	500	750	500
Max road speed (km/hr)	70	70	80	80	100	60
Protection						
Max hull armour (mm)	?	19	15	9	14	7
Turret armour (mm)	?	23	25	7	7	7
Full CBR system	Yes	Yes	Yes	Yes	Yes	No

Artillery Characteristics

	Self-Propelled			*Towed Guns*		
	2S1	**2S3**	**S-23**	**D-20**	**D-30**	**M-1946**
Length (m)	7.30	7.80	10.49	8.14	5.4	11.73
Height (m)	2.40	2.70	2.62	2.76	1.66	2.55
Width (m)	2.85	3.2	2.99	2.03	1.95	2.06
Weight (tonne)	16	23	20.4	5.65	3.15	8.45
Elevation (—/+)	3°/70°	3°/65°	2°/50°	5°/63°	7°/70°	$2\frac{1}{2}$°/45°
Traverse (in firing position)	360°	360°	44°	60°	360°	50°
Crew	4	4	15	10	7	9
Max range, normal rd (km)	15.3	18.5	30.4	18.5	15.3	27.5
Max range, RAP round (km)	n/a	n/a	43.8	n/a	n/a	n/a
Burst rate of fire	5	5	2	5	7	5
Sustained rate of fire	2	2	1	2	3	2

Below left:
The M-1938 122mm howitzer. Produced in huge quantities during the war it is still found in some category III divisions.

Below:
East German D-20 152mm howitzers parade down Berlin's Karl Marx Allee. *ADN*

Top right:
The M-1943 120mm mortar has been used by regimental mortar batteries since the war.

Far top right:
The M-1952 240mm mortar, a massive weapon capable of firing nuclear or conventional rounds 10km. Behind it, seemingly dwarfed, a 160mm mortar.

Right:
The 'Big Fred' artillery locating radar is mounted on an MT-LB.
via C. F. Foss

Far right:
The BM-21 multiple rocket launcher can fire its 40 122mm rockets in under a minute.

Below right:
The T-12 100mm anti-tank gun serves in many divisions, a sign of the continued Soviet faith in this type of weapon.
US Army via C. F. Foss

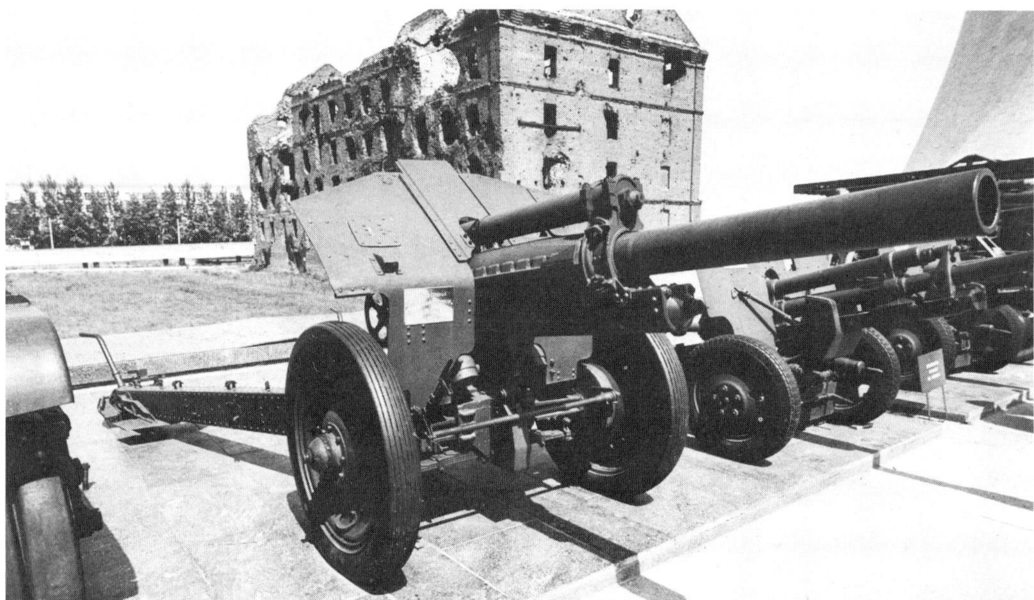

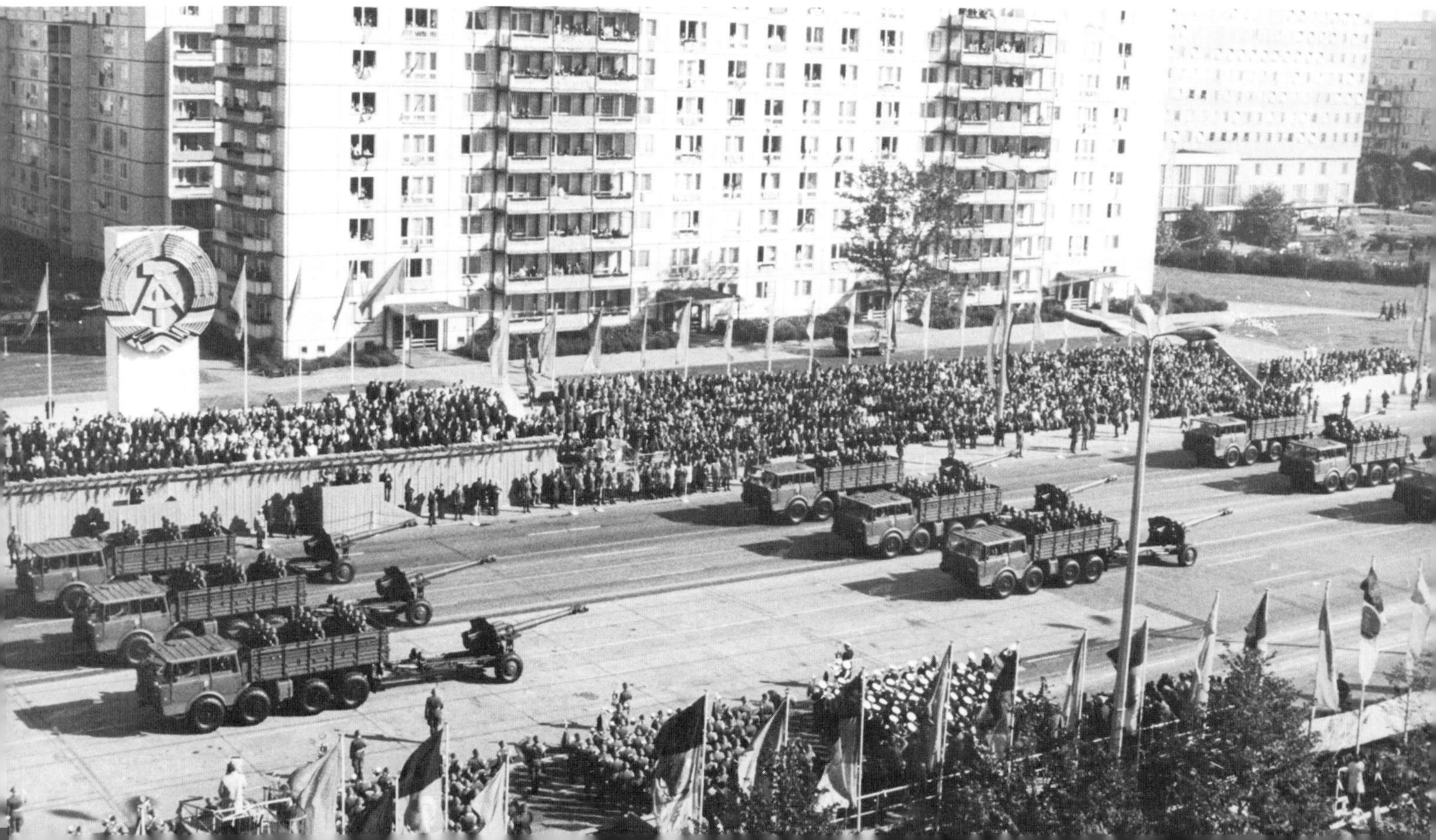

Above:
'Frog-7' tactical nuclear missiles of the Hungarian Army.
via C. F. Foss

Right:
The highly mobile 'Scud-B' missile is mounted on a transporter built at the MAZ factory in Minsk. *Tass*

Below right:
'Scaleboard' front-level tactical nuclear missiles. These have been replaced in GSFG and the Central Group by the SS-23. *Novosti*

86

divisional weapons use nuclear warheads of 20-40KT and can also be fitted with high explosive devices. Army level nuclear firepower consists of 'Scud' brigades equipped with a dozen TELs each. Early 'Scud-A' missiles were mounted on JSIII-derived vehicles and serve in some cadre and NSWP units. Most Soviet armies now have the 'Scud-B' mounted on the impressive Maz-543 vehicle. It has a range of 280km and is being replaced by a system called 'Scud-C' or SS-23. Army level 'Scud' systems use 40-100KT warheads. Frontal commanders have the 'Scaleboard' system, in service since 1967, which fires a one-megaton warhead to a distance of 800km. Larger missiles such as the SS-20 are held by the Strategic Rocket Forces but might be placed under the C-in-Cs of TVDs in war. 'Frogs' and 'Scuds' have been fired in anger in both the Arab-Israeli and Gulf Wars fitted with conventional warheads. Their accuracy was hopeless and they were unable to hit targets as big as airbases. For this reason the Soviets would probably fire them only with nuclear warheads.

Reconnaissance of nuclear and chemical contaminated areas is performed by units equipped with BRDM-RKH vehicles. These have devices to measure toxicity levels and a system for planting flags to mark clear paths through contaminated areas. There are also a whole family of systems used for rapid decontamination of men and vehicles. The TMS-65 features a MiG-15 jet engine mounted on the back of a Ural-375 truck, and works rather like a giant aerosol. In addition to this defensive equipment they also hold stocks of chemical weapons and systems for their delivery. Chemical stocks include non-persistent and persistent choking, blistering and nerve agents. Some have to be inhaled and and others are absorbed through the skin. The most effective means for delivering these substances are multiple rocket launchers and tanks carried by aircraft. Some Soviet theorists have written enthusiastically about the use of chemical weapons, but more sober minds must realise that the use of such weapons, like nuclear ones, carries the near certainty of retaliation.

Air defence is entrusted to a whole family of systems designed to form an interlocking net. Regimental air defence is based on ZSU-23-4s and SA-9s on BRDM vehicles, and man-portable SA-7s. SA-13 missiles are mounted on an MT-LB chassis for better mobility and are replacing SA-9s in some units; they have also been seen at Kabul airport in Afghanistan. Divisional anti-aircraft regiments use SA-6 'Gainful' and SA-8 'Gecko' missiles or S-60 anti-aircraft guns. The ramjet-powered SA-6 is an outstanding design associated with the Straight Flush radar — the combination caused the Israeli Air Force considerable losses in 1973. The SA-8 deployed in GSFG since 1979 is noteworthy for having its search and tracking radars mounted on each missile-firing vehicle. Unlike other Soviet SAMs each SA-8 launcher is equipped with its own sophisticated suite of radars and electronics.

These vehicles, designated *Zenitniy Raketniy Kompleks*, or anti-aircraft missile system, can be brought into action quickly and unlike other SAM batteries are not dependent on radar vehicles which can be knocked out by anti-radiation missiles: it is nevertheless a highly expensive solution. Both SA-6 and SA-8 are subject to countermeasures, and in the Bekaa Valley in 1982 the Israelis devastated Syrian air defences with the loss of only two aircraft. Army air defence is entrusted to SA-4 'Ganef' systems. The high technology SA-11 has been deployed in limited numbers, in places on a basis of one unit being integrated into a SA-6 battery. A new high altitude system, SA-10, which may well replace SA-4, is also being deployed in limited numbers. Theatre forces will include further batteries of SA-5 'Gammon', SA-2 'Guideline' and SA-3 'Goa' systems. All of these air defence resources have been placed under the organisational mantle of the PVO troops since 1981.

Engineering troops are equipped with a great deal of specialised equipment, much of it associated with the crossing of water obstacles. The K-61 amphibious transporter can carry three tons of equipment or 50 men at 10km/hr. The more modern PTS-M vehicle can carry 70 men or 10 tons of cargo. Both are held by divisional and army engineer units. GSP heavy ferries (two vehicles form a single ferry) are also held by divisions and are usually used to carry tanks. In battle, once first echelon forces ferried across rivers by K-61s, PTS-Ms and GSPs have secured the crossing, pontoon bridges will be constructed for support elements. TMM bridges can be built into 40m Class 60 spans in an hour under ideal conditions. Larger Class 60 bridges up to 120m long are constructed with PMP pontoon bridges. PMP sections are carried on Kraz-255 trucks and it would take an hour to deploy a divisional set of 16 units. The ingenious PMP system may also be used to build large rafts.

The IMR (Combat Engineer Tractor) is based on the T-54/5 chassis. It has a bulldozer blade and a large mechanical arm designed for clearing obstacles under fire. Another vehicle derived from the T-54/5 has large mine rollers at the front, and no turret, and is being used to clear routes in Afghanistan. BTR-50s with two rocket-propelled explosive-filled hoses mounted in boxes on the rear decks are also in service in the mine-clearance role. KMT-5 mine rollers can also be issued to tank units for minefield breaching operations.

The large GMZ (M-1977) vehicle, based on the SA-4 launch vehicle, carries 200 mines and can lay them at a rate of eight (on the surface) or four (buried) per minute. Lower readiness units use PMR-3 minelayers (similar to the British bar mine system) towed by BTR-152s or Ural trucks. Anti-personnel mines have been sown extensively by helicopters in Afghanistan. The BAT engineer vehicle (based on an AT-T gun tractor) is used to clear pathways and dig gun and tank emplacement. BTM and MDK diggers are used for trench and emplacements digging.

Warsaw Pact weapons production outside the USSR is centred in Poland and Czechoslovakia. Poland produces tanks (T-55 and now T-72), self-propelled guns (2S1) and APCs (OT-6 and OT-64). Czech products include tanks (formerly T-55, now T-72), the MT-55 bridgelayer, BMPs and the RM-70 multiple rocket launcher. The Hungarians produce the FUG-70 scout car which is also used by East German paramilitary forces. Alone among NSWP countries the Rumanians manufacture the BTR-60 under licence, designated TAB-72.

Examination of Soviet weapons deliveries to NSWP countries over the past 20 years illustrates the changing pecking order in Eastern Europe. In the 1950s and 1960s Poles had the first priority in receiving new equipment, but in the 1970s this has fallen to the East Germans. The GDR has received priority shipments of T-72 tanks, Mil-24 gunships and SA-4 missiles. The northern tier has consistently received better equipment than Hungary, Bulgaria and Rumania in the southern tier.

Soviet client states in the Middle East have often been supplied with new weapons before the NSWP states. Late in 1983 for example

Above right:
Pairs of GSP vehicles join to form a ferry capable of carrying a tank across a river at 7km/hr. A new assault ferry designated M-2 is coming into service.

Right:
The TMM bridge is held at regimental level: a 40m span can be built in an hour. Tass

Below:
PMP bridging sections under assembly. The divisional holding of 18 sections can be built into a 118m long Class 60 bridge in under an hour. ADN

Syria alone possessed more T-72 tanks than all the NSWP countries put together. Middle Eastern states (particularly Syria, Libya and Iraq) have also received surface-to-air missiles well in advance of eastern Europe. This practice doubtless causes grumblings among Pact generals, including Soviet ones. It is generally assumed that the Soviets have been unwilling to provide NSWP states with certain weapons, but it is equally possible that in many cases (for example the T-62) the eastern Europeans simply didn't want them. It is interesting to note that the NSWP states have received 'Frog' and 'Scud' missiles. These weapons are ineffective with conventional warheads and the Soviets neither need nor want to supply them with nuclear ones. Why they hold these weapons is therefore something of a mystery. Perhaps they are maintained for use by the Russians in war, or alternatively they serve a symbolic role taking pride of place in the various national day parades.

It is often stated that the standardisation of equipment confers decisive operational and logistical advantages. In fact the real amount of standardisation within the WTO is only marginally better than that in NATO, but for different reasons. Whereas within NATO there are a number of states producing different designs, in eastern Europe only the USSR really introduces new hardware. It does so at such a rate that the end result is a similar number of different systems. NATO countries use three principal tank gun calibres (105mm, 120mm and 120mm smooth bore) and so does the Warsaw Pact (100mm, 115mm and 125mm).

Above left:
An MDK-2 trench digging engineer tractor. *via C. F. Foss*

Left:
The RM-70 multiple rocket launcher is produced in Czechoslovakia. *ADN*

Eastern Europe fields five different personnel carriers (BTR-50, BTR-152, BTR-60, BMP and OT-64) with substantial automotive differences. Artillery is standardised with the 122mm and 152mm calibres predominating, but NATO has also had success in this field.

Production of support vehicles is extensive within the NSWP states, particularly in Czechoslovakia and the East Germans (Ernst Gruber trucks), there being an obvious recognition that the Soviets are unable to provide for the civil and military requirements of so many countries. Even the states of the southern tier satisfy a substantial part of their own requirement for motor transport: Hungary's Csepel and Raba works and Rumania with Carpati and Bucegi trucks. Although some of these locally-produced vehicles are derived from Russian ones there are still substantial differences in the transport of most of these countries. In both combat and support equipment there is less standardisation in the Pact than is generally thought in the West.

6. THE WAR MACHINE IN ACTION

★

CZECHOSLOVAKIA AND AFGHANISTAN

Czechoslovakia

Although the Soviet Army did very little fighting in August 1968 the intervention in Czechoslovakia is an important example of the war machine in action for it involved large scale mobilisation of forces in the western USSR. It was the only time in recent years that the Warsaw Pact went through the motions of preparing for a war in Europe.

The intervention of WTO forces was triggered by the activities of the renegade Czechoslovak leader Alexander Dubcek and his supporters. In April 1968 Dubcek and his progressive faction edged a number of old hard-liners out of the Praesidium (equivalent of the Politburo). They then instituted an Action Programme of reforms relaxing some and implementing other measures designed to give socialism a 'human face'. The least acceptable development for the Russians was that the Party lost its monopoly on political debate. The upheaval extended throughout Czechoslovak society — even the armed forces became involved in public soul-searching. Staff of the Klement Gottwald Military Academy issued a memorandum which questioned the basic direction of Czech military policy and pointed to neutrality outside the Pact as one possible course of action.

Throughout the Prague spring a stream of senior Soviet political and military figures visited the country on fact-finding missions. These included Marshal Iakubovskii, C-in-C of the Warsaw Pact, and Gen Yepishev, head of the MPA. Yepishev played a critical role in the eventual Soviet decision to intervene. As Chief of the MPA he was uniquely placed, having the trust of both political and military leaders. Since his appointment in 1962 he had led the struggle to cement Pact unity and he saw all of his gains being placed in jeopardy by the Czech leadership. He was an important advocate of military intervention.

From May 1968 troop movements were begun to put pressure on the leaders in Prague. On 30 May several thousand Soviet troops arrived unannounced in Bohemia for exercises. Simultaneously other manoeuvres began throughout the western USSR, GDR and Poland, codenamed 'Sumava'. Their purpose was to remind Dubcek of the military option and also to prepare the Soviet Army for action.

During 'Sumava' selected category II and III divisions in the Baltic, Byelorussian and Carpathian MDs received thousands of reservists. Further personnel were drafted in from the Moscow, Kiev and Odessa districts. In many of the category III formations readiness was extremely poor.

Although the 'Sumava' exercises ended officially on 30 June the reservists were kept in uniform and the units continued training. On 17 July the CPSU Central Committee gave its approval for military action if necessary. A special theatre level staff group was formed in the Carpathian MD. It remained quite separate from the district staff and was responsible for staff planning for the operation. Before such action could take place there would have to be huge movements of troops and supplies.

On 24 July the Warsaw Pact forces begun 'Nieman', a logistic and communications exercise under the command of Gen

S. Mariakhin, Chief of Rear Services. War stocks of equipment and ammunition were issued to units and large scale troop movements begun to transfer the forces to concentration areas close to the Czech border. It was at this stage in the operation that thousands of 'civilian' trucks registered with the Army under the *autokolomka* system were commandeered by the Army to make up for its lack of motor transport.

Meanwhile at Cierna, a town on the Czechoslovak/USSR border, the last political moves were played during 29-31 July. Dubcek and Brezhnev met face to face and the Soviets left the conference in an apparently conciliatory mood. This was in fact a grand act of political deception designed to allay Czech fears of an intervention. The Kremlin had determined that military action would have to be taken before the 14th Congress of the Czechoslovak Communist Party which was expected to give enthusiastic backing to Dubcek.

The 'Nieman' exercise was extended to involve units in the GDR and Poland. By 9 August, when 'Nieman' officially ended, most of the Warsaw Pact forces were at their jumping off points for the invasion. The 11th Guards Army had been moved hundreds of miles from Kaliningrad on the Baltic coast to southern Poland. It was made up of several category I and II divisions drawn from the Baltic and Byelorussian MDs. It appears that nearly all of the category III divisions which had been brought up to strength were unready to take part in the operation. 11th Guards Army was joined in Poland by the 8th Guards Tank Army of the Carpathian MD.

During 'Nieman' two armies of the Group of Soviet Forces Germany were also readied for action. These were the 20th Guards Army and 1st Guards Tank Army. There were a number of contingents from other WTO countries, the largest of which was a Polish army of four divisions (only two of which actually entered the country). This army was commanded by Lt-Gen Florian Siwicki and was based on the headquarters of the Silesian MD. The East German contribution was of elements of two divisions: 11th Motor Rifle, which came under the command of the 1st Guards Tank Army, and 7th Tank under the 20th Guards Army. The Hungarians provided several regiments and the Bulgarians a brigade. These southern forces were formed into a group smaller than a front and larger than an army, and code-named 'Balaton'.

The period from the end of 'Nieman' to the invasion itself saw a great increase of signals traffic. Once again this was called an exercise 'Elektronika-68'. Around 10 August the overall command of the operation, which had in the preparatory stages rested with Iakubovskii's Warsaw Pact HQ, was taken over by the Danube High Command, a TVD headquarters based on the separate planning staff set up earlier in the Carpathian District. Army-Gen Pavlovskii, 1st Deputy C-in-C of the Ground Forces, was appointed in charge. A Central Front was formed under Col-Gen Mayorov consisting of three Soviet armies and the Polish forces. The Carpathian MD

Left:
During the 'Sumava' exercise troops were massed near Czechoslovakia's borders.
Novosti

became the Carpathian Front under the command of Col-Gen Bisyarin.

Pavlovskii's task was to seize the country as quickly as possible, as the Kremlin felt there was some risk of Western intervention. The quickest way to take the key centres of population was with airborne forces, and the Danube High Command was assigned two air assault divisions and five of the eight heavy aircraft divisions of Military Transport Aviation (VTA). During the period before the invasion a number of Soviet staffs actually travelled along their invasion routes instructing commanders on their precise duties and itineraries. During the 'Nieman' exercise much of the Czech Army's ammunition had been moved out of the country and given to Pact forces.

On 17 August a team of KGB Special Forces arrived in Prague to co-ordinate the seizure of the capital. They were assisted in their preparations by elements of the Czech Ministry of the Interior which were loyal to the Soviets. The invasion was launched at 23.00hrs on 20 August. Two An-24 aircraft landed at Prague Ruzyne airport with KGB Special Forces teams which joined their colleagues as pathfinders for the intervention force. The first An-12 plane landed at 02.00hrs and disgorged members of the 103rd Guards Air Assault Division, who quickly seized the airport. At the same time

heliborne paratroops were landing in Bratislava near the Hungarian border.

KGB men in embassy cars led the paratroops from Ruzyne to downtown Prague. By 03.30hrs they had reached the Central Committee building. Meanwhile Czech secret police secured the radio station and surrounded the foreign embassies to prevent them from being used as refuges. (During the 1956 Soviet intervention in Hungary a number of prominent government figures had done this causing the Kremlin some embarrassment.) By the early hours of the morning, already confident of success, the Russians and East Germans were broadcasting news of the intervention to the world. Soviet paratroops burst into the offices of the Czech government and seized the cabinet members, who were in late night session. By six in the morning elements of 20th Guards Army were arriving in Prague, having marched through the night. The 1st Guards Tank Army set a cracking pace passing through Pilzen at 06.00hrs on its way south. It had the mission of cutting the routes to the west so as to prevent any exodus from the country. Even though these forward elements moved at great speed with vehicles closer together than under normal tactical conditions, there were elements of the intervention force still entering the country 36 hours afterwards.

The Soviets dropped tons of chaff to disrupt radars and communications and airborne elements seized command installations, all of which helped to prevent any resistance by the Czech Army. It is difficult to see what the Czech Army could have done, as it had to guard land borders of 2,625km. It had in any case been completely wrong-footed by the apparently optimistic outcome of the Cierna talks.

As the country awoke to find itself host to 250,000 guests from the fraternal countries there were a number of attacks on Warsaw Pact troops, and demonstrations. These consisted of little more than occasional sniping and some petrol bombs. It is estimated that Soviet losses during the entire operation did not exceed 150, many of whom were killed in accidents. Guards Lt-Gen Velichko, commander of the 20th Guards Army, was put in charge of Prague and northern Bohemia, and he imposed a curfew and other restrictions. The Soviets sought to gain approval for their actions from conservative Czechoslovak communists, but this took longer than expected; according to some this was a victory for Czech passive resistance. The fact that the Czechs were talking about passive resistance was however merely a measure of the humiliation which they had already suffered.

This operation provided a number of

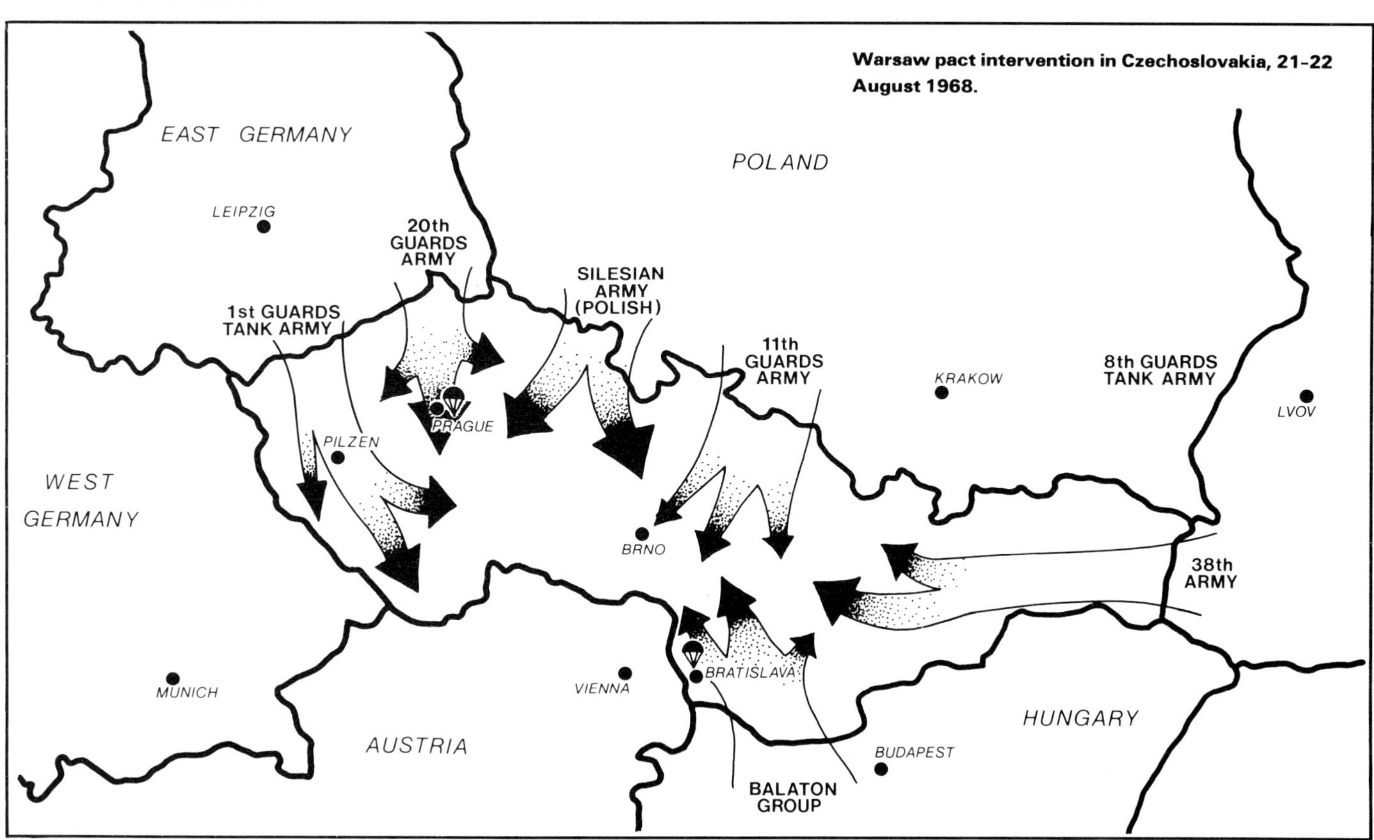

Above left:
The task of seizing many key objectives fell to the highly trained Air Assault Forces. *via C. F. Foss*

Left:
In a matter of days around one quarter of a million Warsaw Pact troop entered Czechoslovakia, ending Dubcek's attempt at socialism with a human face.
Associated Press via C. F. Foss

Below left:
A unit of the 20th Guards Army on the outskirts of Prague.
Associated Press via C. F. Foss

important military lessons. The Soviet Army moved with impressive speed and efficiency, albeit under non-tactical conditions, but we must remember that it took at least two months to prepare itself. The category III formations failed to measure up and most were left in camp. The crucial missions were entrusted to the Air Assault Forces and troops drawn from GSFG — all category I units. The WTO forces found themselves desperately short of transport and had to take over thousands trucks, which resulted in a disaster for Russian harvesting. The formation of the Danube High Command marked the rebirth of the theatre level of command and also highlighted the operational redundancy of the Warsaw Pact structure. Polish, East German, Hungarian and Bulgarian forces were directly integrated into the Soviet Army at divisional, army and front levels. According to some reports the Russian troops were told that they were on their way to fight NATO troops in West Germany; if true this teaches us that Soviet troops would march into NATO countries if ordered to do so without hesitation.

Afghanistan

The conflict in Afghanistan undoubtedly offers the best example of the war machine in action. Whilst many Westerners have tried to characterise the struggle as Russia's Vietnam it certainly is not. The Soviets have launched very few major offensives, and are clearly prepared to accept the comparatively light casualties that the disunited and largely incompetent Afghan resistance is able to inflict. Since the Soviet intervention there has been some extension of government control over the country although large areas are still the domain of the mujahadeen (Holy Fighters).

The People's Democratic Party (PDP) came to power in April 1978 following a coup d'état. It styled itself as a Marxist party which was to bring revolutionary change to Afghan society. It can be argued with some justification that Afghan society was in need of revolutionary change — 90% of its 18million people are illiterate, and most of them lived under a feudal social structure dominated by the mullahs. But the PDP was badly split between rival factions, most importantly the Parcham headed by Barbrak Karmal, and the Khalq under the leadership of Nur Mohammed Taraki. In July 1978 Taraki was purged unceremoniously to be ambassador in Czechoslovakia. Taraki himself was ousted by a coup on 15 September 1979 by Hafizullah Amin.

Traditionally the localities in Afghanistan have taken little notice of central government anyway, and with constant in-fighting in Kabul they took even less. Resistance groups sprung up, bolstered by defections from the faction-riven army. Throughout 1979 government's control of the countryside deteriorated rapidly. By the time the USSR sent its troops in, 90% of rural Afghanistan was no longer under Kabul's control. Central administration in these areas collapsed to be supplanted by a whole variety of rapidly burgeoning guerilla parties. Although attempts were made to unify these movements, and many have been made since, only limited successes have been achieved, notably the June 1979 grouping of nine movements into the 'National Rescue Front'. The mujahadeen have proved as resistant to central control by guerrillas as they have to central control by communists.

Soviet involvement in the country dated from before the 1978 'April Revolution' and had given the country much of its road system among other things. By 1978 Afghanistan was already the fourth largest recipients of Soviet aid, and as the government found itself being forced out of the countryside this assistance became more and more military in character. An important landmark in Soviet military involvement was the March 1979 seizure of Herat in the west of the country by rebels. It was symptomatic of the depths to which the Kabul regime's fortunes had sunk that the 17th Division, when ordered to fight the guerillas, mutinied and changed sides, giving the rebels heavy weapons from its armouries. During the mayhem a number of Soviet advisors and their wives and children were captured and cut to pieces by the mob. No government in the East or West can be expected to ignore such barbarism, and the Kremlin proved to be no exception.

Early in April 1979 the Afghans received a visit from Army-Gen Yepishev, who the reader will recall made a visit to Czechoslovakia shortly before the Soviet intervention in that country. As a result of his visit shipments of arms to the Democratic Republic of Afghanistan (DRA) were stepped up, including 100 T-62 tanks and 12 Mil-24 helicopter gunships. In June 1979 a further 18 Mil-24s were delivered, and these, along with a number of jets, were flown mainly by Soviet pilots. Attacks on Shindand airbase (April 1979) and Bagram airbase

(June 1979) resulted in the committal of a number of small sub-units (company strength) for the defence of installations in September. Whereas in March there had only been 1,000 Soviet advisors in the country by November 1979 there were 3,500. Throughout the summer of 1979 the military situation got worse and it was decided in the Kremlin that plans should be made for an intervention in the DRA.

The first step, as in previous interventions, was the establishment of a special planning group drawn from the General Staff. This group, believed to have numbered around 50, visited Afghanistan in mid-August 1979 with Army-Gen Pavlovskii at its head. From what they saw and from further information provided by Maj-Gen Gorelov (head of the military mission) they can have been under no illusions either as to the scale of the insurrection or of the colossal military effort that would be required to tame the mountainous country. It must have been clear even then that the Kremlin would never send the kind of forces required (often estimated at 500,000 men) to crush all opposition: from the beginning then their plans must have acknowledged the physical control of the whole country would not be the mission of the intervention force.

It is difficult to date the actual decision in Moscow to intervene, but steps to top up the category II and category III and formations were under way from early November 1979. There was every indication that without major assistance the Kabul regime would fall. The Soviets feared that in the wake of such a collapse the country would be gripped by the same kind of anarchy that followed the fall of the Shah of Iran. There was a risk that this might in turn pose problems among the central Asian minorities of the southern USSR. Soviet investment in the DRA had already been considerable and clearly the Kremlin regarded the existence of a friendly government in Kabul as an important factor in the security of its southern border. The Amin regime in Kabul did not prove altogether co-operative and the Soviets decided that it would have to be replaced by a more pliant one headed by the exiled Karmal and his Parcham faction. Amin's government had relied on repressive tactics, imprisoning and torturing thousands, and as his standing in the country sunk lower and lower he became more and more of a liabiiity to Moscow.

And so the invasion plans were set in motion. From the last week of November US diplomats and other foreigners were refused permission to visit Soviet central Asia. Large troop movements took place: 201 Motor Rifle Division moved from Dushanbe to Termez and 66 Motor Rifle to Kushka. Bridging units prepared their equipment for a crossing of the Amu Darya (Oxus River) which divides the two states. Reservists were called up, including officers; many of the latter were given technical and political tasks. To avoid more obvious national troop movements mainly local men were mobilised giving the divisions (initially, at least) a distinctly central Asian 'flavour'. These formations entered the DRA with a shortage of specialists and technical grades, at around two-thirds of established strength. Aviation

Left:
Forces of the Turkestan district formed the bulk of the intervention force assembled in the Southern theatre in November and December 1979.
Tass

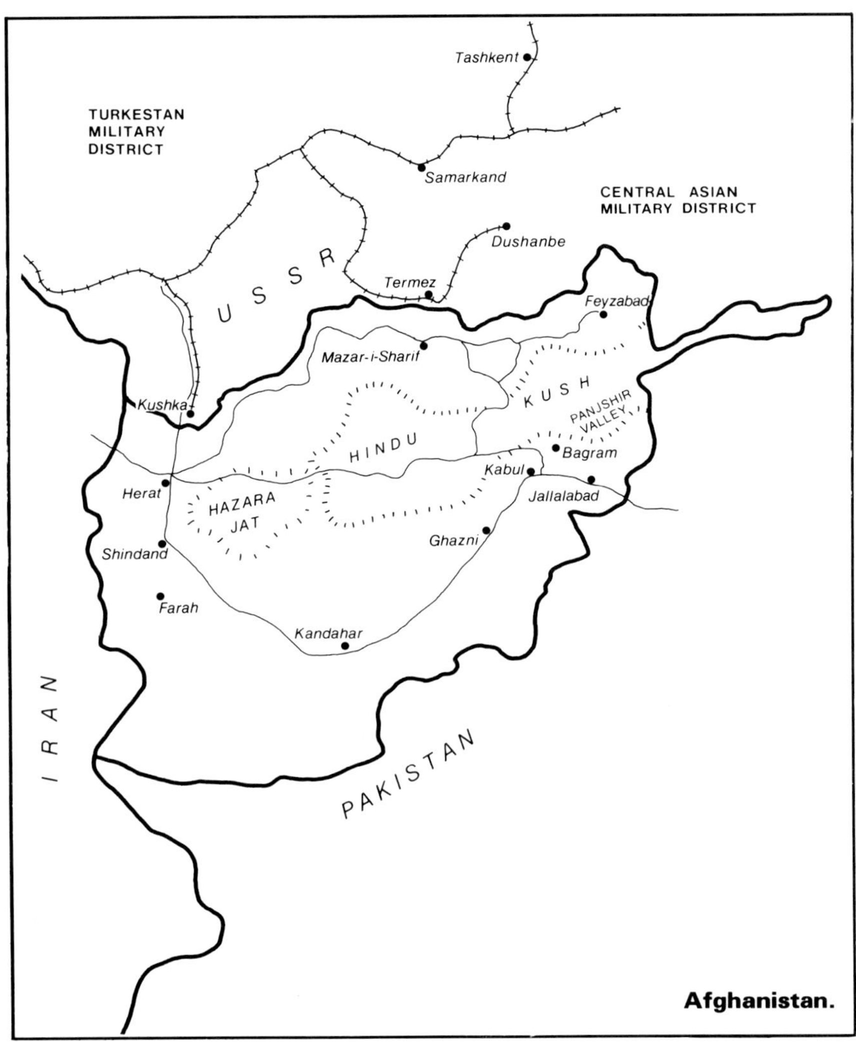

Afghanistan.

from Herat around the Haza Rajat mountains to Kandahar. The other led to the capital via the Salang Pass. The safety of the Salang Pass was open to question as the guerillas had successfully attacked it, blowing up an important bridge in September 1979.

One advantage which the Soviet forces would enjoy which the Tsar's generals in 1877 did not was that they could employ airborne troops to seize targets in depth quickly and efficiently. As in the Prague operation the key task of taking the seat of political power fell to the VDV — the Air Assault Forces. A VDV task force of five rifle regiments, an artillery regiment and other support units was formed under the command of Major-Gen Moussa Yevanov, a talented commander of Uzbeck origin. These five rifle regiments were probably drawn one each from 103rd Guards Air Assault (which arrived on 7 December), 104th Guards Air Assault (from the Transcaucasus MD) and three from the 105th Guards which was stationed close to the DRA in the neighbouring Turkestan MD.

In December the Southern TVD was activated with the First Deputy Minister of Defence, Marshal Sergei Sokolov, in charge. His forward command centre in Termez was activated as the headquarters 40th Army. The first stage of the operation was put into operation on 19 December when the air assault regiment moved from Bagram into the Salang Pass and secured this vital routeway to Kabul. Forty-eight hours later Yevanov began moving his second regiment into the DRA. The VDV task force concentrated at Kabul and Bagram airfields until 27 December when the main forces were ready to cross the frontier.

The Soviet plan involved replacing Amin with a new Karmal government that would attempt to rectify past mistakes and rally the armed forces whose morale had been crumbling steadily. From the beginning however the idea of packaging Karmal and his Parcham followers as the party of reconciliation was a problematical one. The mujahadeen and mullah's would regard him as 'just another communist' and the Afghan army officer corps which had been largely staffed by Taraki and Khalq men would have no great love for a Parcham leader. Despite these risks the Soviets felt that a new Karmal government of reconciliation was worth the risk. Should this gamble fail Sokolov was moving three more motor rifle divisions to the frontier.

The movement of forces into Afghanistan

elements were the next to be put in place, and the headquarters for the operation which had been set up in Termez soon had two heavy lift divisions of the VTA under its command. The Air Assault Forces alert formation, 103rd Guards in Vietbsk (Byelorussian MD), sent its spearhead regiment to Bagram airbase on 7 December; its mission became apparent later.

Whereas during the Czechoslovak operation formations were moved to their start positions by the Warsaw Pact staff, in the case of Afghanistan this task was performed by the Organisation and Mobilisation Main Directorate of the General Staff. In Termez Pavlovski had been replaced at the head of the planning group by Army-Gen Valentin Varrennikov who had arrived from commanding the Carpathian MD late in November. The plan that the group drew up for the seizure of the country owed much to one drafted in 1877 by the Russian Imperial Staff. It emphasised that the rugged terrain would canalise movement in two main directions. The westerly route would take the Soviet forces along the newly improved road was conducted with speed and vigour. The 66 and 346 Motor Rifle Divisions moved from Kushka south to Herat and Kandahar respectively; 360 Motor Rifle in company with 201 Motor Rifle drove to Kabul, with the latter then proceeding to Jallalabad. The Air Assault Forces were directed to their targets by KGB and GRU Special Forces. The activities of these forces were co-ordinated by Lt-Gen Paputin, a Deputy Interior Minister who had been sent to Kabul. Amin and his followers were at the Darulaman Palace outside Kabul where they had gone supposedly on Soviet advice 'for safety'. The palace was assaulted by paratroopers and Amin and his guards and family eliminated. The attack on the palace apparently became necessary because Paputin had failed to persuade Amin to 'come quietly'. This failure proved a political embarrassment to the Kremlin and Paputin is said to have committed suicide.

Karmal denounced the previous regime and took a number of important steps to try and gain popularity and reconciliation. On 28 December he made a speech affirming his respect for 'the holy Islamic tradition, for family folk and national traditions'. He persuaded Abdul Aziz Sadiq, chairman of the council of religious elders, to declare his support for the new regime. Karmal's new cabinet included a number of prominent Khalq faction members, notably the First Deputy Prime Minister. Government propaganda denounced Amin as an anti-Islamic puppet of the CIA and declared the new regime and its Soviet backers to have the true interests of Islam at heart. On 1 January Karmal announced a big amnesty and 9,000 political prisoners were released from jails across the country. It was hoped that all of these measures would undermine guerila support and gain the backing of the Khalq. It was a bold plan which was doomed to fail.

The Afghan Army was split rather than unified by the intervention and desertion which had always been a problem reached spectacular proportions. At Jallalabad for example an entire brigade of 2,000 men joined the rebels. The Afghan 8th Division mutinied at Kargh. During the first year of the Soviet's presence it is arguable that the Afghan Army was more of a menace to them than the guerillas. A number of mutinies brought heavy fighting with Soviet units, and the Afghan Army — unlike the mujahadeen — had both heavy weapons and some idea of how to use them. A case in point was the mutiny of the 14th Armoured Division at

Ghazni which erupted in July 1980 when Karmal replaced the Khalq faction commander with one from Parcham. Soviet and loyal Afghan units were forced to retake Ghazni at some cost in casualties because the rebellion threatened the important ring road which connects the major towns in the country.

It was apparent to Sokolev within a couple of weeks of the intervention that with local friendly forces disintegrating fast he would have to commit his reserves and prepare for a long stay. And so on 15 January the 5th, 16th and 54th Motor Rifle Divisions began entering the country, and the 40th Army HQ was moved to Bagram. Having failed in their gamble to win all-party support for Karmal, and with the Afghan Army falling apart, the Soviets saw no choice other than the continued support of the Kabul regime. Withdrawal would be politically unacceptable, unless the mujahadeen could be neutralised by a deal with religious leaders and the Pakistani government. Lt-Gen V. M. Mikhailov, formerly First Deputy Commander of the Turkestan MD, was given command of the 40th Army. Mikhailov's strategy involved the holding of a number of important towns and the roads that connected them. Soviet forces were stationed outside towns and initially made little attempt to control what went on inside them leading to guerilla claims to have 'taken' towns like Herat and Kandahar. By and large his brief did not include going out to fight the mujahadeen in the countryside — this job was left to the depleted Afghan Army. Only in Kunar and Paktia provinces (on the Pakistani border) where the Kabul forces had effectively disintegrated and the guerillas made their greatest gains did the Soviets attempt to fight on a large (divisional) scale in 1980. A number of facts point to the

relatively minor combat role of Soviet ground forces. Firstly the mujahadeen failed to produce a single living Russian prisoner during 1980, and even if we take it for granted that they killed them all it is worth noting that they only produced a handful of ID cards. Secondly, during that first year the guerillas captured no more than 50 or 60 AK-74 rifles which are used exclusively by the Russians. Even today they have so few AK-74s that ownership of one is considered a status symbol among the guerillas.

Soviet air forces have been more active, often striking at targets in rural and mountainous areas. The bombing of villages has resulted in many civilian casualties and an enormous flow of refugees to Pakistan both of which serve the purposes of the mujahadeen. In many cases the bombing has been indiscriminate or ineffective because the pilots, wary of ground fire, have been too timid to bomb from tactically realistic altitudes. The Soviet flyers have experienced problems with their bombs, with many failing to arm before impact. Travellers in the country report seeing many unexploded bombs. Attempts to solve this problem have included the introduction of retard bombs.

Guerilla activity during 1980 centred on the rugged Pakistani border region. Some also infiltrated from Iran to strike Herat, Kandahar and Shindand. Successes were scored in a number of ambush operations notably by guerillas attacking the Kabul to Pul-i-Khumri (where the Soviets have an important logistics centre) road from havens in the Panjshir valley. Most guerillas seem however to have displayed a lack of tactical know-how, having neither the martial skills nor the idealism often attributed to them in the Western media. Most of them are Pathans who according to Nick Downie (a former SAS man turned film-maker who has made a number of trips to the DRA and other guerilla wars) possess virtually none of the qualities required to make good guerilla fighters. Lofty ideological beliefs do not seem to have prevented many of the tribesmen from joining the well-paid government militias. Many of the Pathans make their living by collecting weapons and equipment from Afghan Army deserters and selling them to the Pakistani government across the border. The Pakistanis offer them high prices because they are afraid that the weapons might otherwise find their way to their own discontented Baluchi minority.

With the situation in Jallalabad stabilised somewhat in 1981 Mikhailov turned his attention to those mujahadeen who posed the only real threat to the supply of his forces, the men of the Panjshir valley. These fighters are led by Ahmadshah Massood, a Tajik, and by 1981 had succeeded in establishing a veritable stronghold in the 80-mile long mountain valley to the northeast of Kabul. 1981 saw a series of attacks on the Panjshir with a fully concerted offensive from 10 September to 30 September. This action seems to have secured the Kabul road for a few months. Just as this offensive was ending, serious trouble was brewing in Herat. During the next few months the Russians clearly felt that they were achieving results in this locality because they broke past silences and made a number of specific claims of casualties. Radio Moscow claimed 600 guerillas killed in October 1981, and 2,200 in February 1982, a direct admission of the scale of the fighting. During early 1982 further operations were conducted in this area, and on 8 April Soviet troops reportedly crossed into Iran in pursuit of guerillas. All of this evidently alarmed the government in Tehran which on 20 May handed over a number of Afghan rebels and restricted their operations from that country.

Throughout 1981-82 attempts were made to rebuild the Afghan Army which by then had shrunk from 80,000 when the Russians arrived to 30,000. Divisional HQs became used more as provincial command staffs for military operations. Provinces were given Operational Battalions charged with prosecuting mobile war in remote areas. The services of villagers around a number of towns were wooed and bought and they were formed into militias. Their task is to seal the towns off from guerrilla activity, and they have been partially successful, forcing the rebels to use bombs in the towns.

1982 also saw repeated attacks on Massood and his band of 3,000 guerillas in

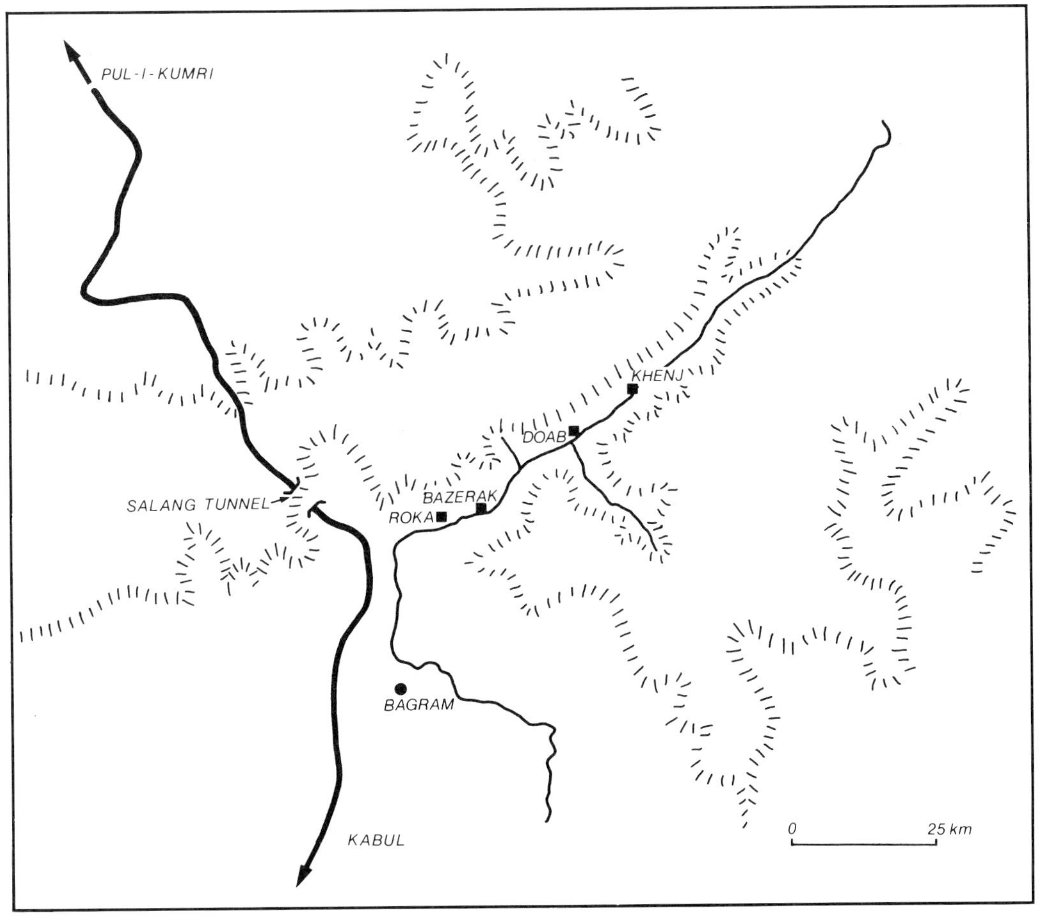

the Panjshir. Massood played host to Western journalists and ran a guerilla training camp, all of which was becoming increasingly embarrassing to Moscow. Undoubtedly the Soviets have seen heavy fighting in the Panjshir; one private, Yuri, wrote home, 'From our company four have already been killed and our *zampolit* Batuyev was blown up by a mine and they hardly found anything left of him ... there's practically nothing left of the third company, they're all either in zinc boxes or the hospital' (this letter was given to British broadcaster Sandy Gall who was in the Panjshir at this time).

The Soviets launched two main offensives in 1982, 'Panjshir 5' (so-called because it represented the fifth concerted push by the Russians) from May to early June, and 'Panjshir 6' from August to September. In both cases the Soviets cordoned the mouth of the valley and then conducted a fire preparation with Su-25 'Frogfoots', MiGs and 'Hind' gunships before pushing an armoured column up the valley. The Soviets committed a motor rifle division to the operation, and when Afghan forces are included disposed of perhaps 20,000 men. Massood's guerilla army was believed to number between 2,000 and 3,000, around 600 of whom were organised into half a dozen 'motoraks' or mobile fighting groups, company strength raiding forces.

On 17 May the Russians landed a reinforced battalion by helicopter deep in the valley near Khenj, and it was immediately attacked. They then pushed a reinforced regiment towards the air-landed force, but this too soon ran into difficulties. Eventually it penetrated to within a few miles of the heliborne force, but lost a company's worth of men and vehicles in another ambush near a town called Doab and failed to link up.

'Panjshir 6' was begun in almost identical fashion with bombing and a heliborne landing near Khenj, but this time the Soviets made numerous attacks against side valleys and defiles which had been used by the guerillas to launch ambushes during 'Panjshir 5'. They succeeded in linking up with the air-landed force and left the valley destroying supplies and buildings. Clearly they had learnt a number of costly lessons in the first offensive, many of which were put right.

As the Soviet presence has worn on the Russian media has carried more stories about the troops in the DRA. On 23 February 1982 *Red Star* published a frank account of life in Afghanistan ending with an emotional exhortation to the men: 'Know friends that you live in every Soviet

heart. The people are proud of you, they love you, they think of you'. Around 30 Hero of the Soviet Union medals have been awarded in Afghanistan, one to a colonel who commanded a gunship helicopter regiment — Yu Pavlov. Pavlov was posted from Afghanistan to GSFG, just one of thousands of Soviet officers who have taken vital combat experience into an army desperately short of this commodity. It will be interesting to see whether an 'Afghanistan clique' formed of officers who have served in this theatre emerges.

Although there have been many small guerilla attacks it would seem that Soviet divisional offensives have occurred in only three regions: the Kunar and Pakhtia during 1980, Herat in 1981-82 and the Panjshir in 1981, 1982 and 1983. Large engagements have also been fought against Afghan Army rebellions, the most recent of which (25th Division in Khost) took place in January 1983. Soviet offensives have been designed to relieve pressure on the routeways and cities, and in the isolated cases where the normally ineffective mujahadeen have presented a threat to dissipate this. They have fought them in a conventional manner, and it is difficult to imagine a war to which the Soviet Army is less well suited, and given this its performance has been acceptable.

The lessons learnt can be summarised as follows. The invasion itself was well planned and executed with the cadre divisions playing the limited roles assigned to them well. The critical missions were undertaken by the well-trained category I airborne regiments. As usual the staff planning and command was of a high quality. Important innovations include the airborne control of close air support and the field testing of new weapons and tactics. As in most guerilla wars it is the junior level of leadership which must be under the most severe test. It is extremely difficult to calculate Soviet casualties — the Pentagon claims 5,000 during the first three years of the invasion. This figure (which is probably too high) can be averaged out at 32 men per week out of a garrison of 79,000. Even with this estimate of casualties it is apparent both that the Soviets do not play the leading combat role, and that the 90,000 mujahadeen claimed by the Americans to be in the field are incapable of inflicting heavy casualties on them. Politically the cost of the intervention has been higher — the attempt to promote Karmal as a leader of national reconciliation failed in a few weeks. The Kremlin is not prepared to suffer the indignity of a withdrawal at the moment, so the Soviet Army will do what is necessary to maintain its position until a political settlement can be reached.

7. REDRAWING THE MAP

★

SCENARIOS FOR WAR

Doctrine, deployment, intelligence, equipment and the quality of command add up to present us with some idea of the Soviet Union's overall war-fighting capability on land. In each theatre of war there would be different prospects for a Russian military success, and these can be examined in turn. There are though many factors in the complex equation of Soviet land power which would remain constant in all theatres such as the quality of manpower, equipment and leadership.

It is impossible to predict the circumstances that might bring the USSR to wage war in Europe but we can be quite certain that whether or not it was the victim or the perpetrator of an aggression it would make every effort to wage an offensive war. As we have already noted this is not because the Kremlin has some inherently aggressive grand design but because offensive tactics 'offer to the Marxist military mind the sole hope of achieving victory . . . tactics based on the defensive would, the Russians believe, be certain to lose such a war' (P. H. Vigor). A number of factors would press the Soviet Army to advance as quickly as possible. Firstly it must gain ground so quickly that enemy decision makers will not have time to make effective use of nuclear weapons. Secondly, historical experience has shown the Russians that if an enemy is allowed to attack first he may gain a decisive advantage, and loss of Soviet lives will be so much the greater, particularly in the nuclear age. Thirdly, underlying tensions in many of the East European states allied to Moscow could pose problems in a drawn-out conflict.

Above left:
Tactical nuclear missiles like these 'Frog-7s' could be used to punch holes in NATO's front line, so that exploitation forces could then motor through causing havoc in rear areas. *Novosti*

Left:
Russian use of nuclear or chemical weapons would almost certainly bring about retaliation in kind by NATO. These tank crews train in hot and uncomfortable protective clothing. *ADN*

War in the West

The Russians' chances of successfully waging war in the West (in the Central European, Southwest European and Northern TVDs) would depend largely on how much military power they could bring to bear, which in turn depends partly on the readiness of their forces. The overriding importance of the European theatre in Soviet strategic thinking can be seen in the high readiness of the groups of forces and modern equipment of second echelon forces in the western USSR. The comparison of a division in GSFG with one in the Siberian or North Caucasus districts (to name but two) reveals such differences in weaponry and training standards that they might as well be in different armies. Broadly there are three major scenarios: a war from a standing start, a partial mobilisation, and complete mobilisation. A war in central Europe might occur after a period of international tension in which both sides had achieved a partial mobilisation. The outbreak of war might follow a mobilisation crisis or 'war scare' (like those before both world wars) in which each side could become convinced that the other is about to launch an attack. It is a dangerous game indeed to play brinkmanship with a political and military leadership that has witnessed first hand the devastation that occurred last time an enemy was allowed to attack first. NATO politicians might well prove reluctant to order military alerts for fear of triggering a pre-emptive strike from the East.

The 'standing start' scenario assumes that there has been no tension, or if there has been that this has not included mobilisation or deployment of forces. It is very difficult to imagine why the USSR would wage a war from a standing start because it does not offer it a very high chance of victory. Past experience has shown us the four stages that the Russians would go through prior to acting: staff planning, troop movement, air movement and activation of a war command structure. A war from a standing start would involve little staff planning (as doubtless this has already been prepared) and only a small amount of air and troop movement. NATO could only have perhaps 48 hours' warning of such activity.

A critical factor, particularly to those of us who live in western Europe, is whether the opening of hostilities would be accompanied

by a nuclear strike. A number of Soviet theorists assume that it would: 'the main destruction of the enemy is carried out at the beginning of an operation with a powerful massive nuclear strike' (Col M. Skovorodkin of the General Staff writing in '*Military Thought*'). Use of perhaps 30 nuclear bursts against key NATO troop concentrations would allow the Soviets to motor through the remnants at great speed. Such a strategy however carries with it a high risk of inviting a nuclear counter-bombardment of the Motherland. It might just work if the Soviet advance was so devastating — and we are talking in terms of reaching the Channel in 48 hours — that there would be nothing for NATO to save by retaliation. Recent evidence (notably late President Brezhnev's insistence that there could be no victor in a nuclear conflict, and the renewed importance of manoeuvre groups which effectively deny both sides the use of nuclear weapons over large areas of the battlefield) is that like NATO the Soviets might try and abstain from using nuclear weapons for as long as possible. Even with use of conventional aviation and artillery the current correlation of military power does not favour the

Warsaw Pact sufficiently to give it a good chance of a quick victory. Successful delaying tactics by the NATO forward screen which allowed the main force to occupy battle positions would force the Soviets to make the kind of breakthrough attacks that require a superiority of forces of 9:1.

They would attempt to break the NATO line and insert manoeuvre groups with operational and strategic objectives. The best points for them to attempt these breakthroughs are on the major corps boundaries, for example where the British and Belgian corps meet. The use of manoeuvre groups probably offers the Soviets a better chance of success in operations launched from a standing start but is not without its problems. Concentration is needed to achieve the breakthroughs required to insert the groups. If NATO forces rallied successfully they could cut the groups off from supporting forces and destroy them with anti-tank weapons and artillery. The use by the Pact of these operational manoeuvre groups and the possible adoption by NATO of a new US doctrine, 'Airland Battle 2000', would result in interpenetration of the belligerent armies and the breakdown of 'front lines' as such.

Right:
East Germany's forces would form part of the first strategic echelon in central Europe. *ADN*

Left:
T-74 on the move: they would form the spearhead of any thrust into western Europe. *Tass*

Right:
A column of BMPs deploys from the line of march. *Novosti*

A limited mobilisation designed to reinforce the groups of forces would stand a higher chance of success, particularly if this reinforcement could be conducted in secrecy. Three fronts could be activated under the Central European GTVD, probably formed from GSFG, Northern and Central Group HQs. Reserves amounting to a further two or three armies could be prepared in the Baltic, Byelorussian and Carpathian districts with very limited mobilisation by using only high readiness formations. They could then surge their forward strengths during one of the biannual troop rotations without causing undue suspicion. This could amount to a further 60,000 troops in GSFG and sufficient to make a number of category II divisions in the western districts up to war strength. These reinforcement measures would have to be screened by a complex plan of deception which would include political reassurances designed to lull Western governments into a false sense of security. Even these limited reinforcement measures would involve the movement of many thousands of vehicles

The probable deployment of forces and main lines of advance on Day 3 of a Warsaw Pact invasion of Western Europe.

and hundreds of thousands of men, and it is hard to believe that these would go undetected. Nevertheless, even in the age of the satellite, strategic surprise is possible. Take for example the Arab attack on Israel in 1973: although the Israeli intelligence services detected the build-up the political leaders failed to act. Likewise the danger for the West is not that a Soviet build-up would remain undetected but that bureaucrats and politicians will either misinterpret or misjudge the intelligence.

If the USSR managed to launch an offensive against a largely unmobilised defence the outlook for NATO could indeed be bleak. The geographical features of the north German plain, Fulda gap and Hof corridor favour particular routes of advance. Without warning the Allied forces would be at their weakest in the north German region and the Soviets could be expected to make their main attacks in this area. 3rd Shock, 2nd Guards Tank, and 8th Guards armies could all be thrown into the first echelon against NATO's Northern Army Group (NORTHAG).

1st Guards Tank Army would motor down the Fulda gap in an attempt to break through the Germans and Americans, perhaps where their two corps meet. The Central Group would use the Hof corridor to attack the US VIIth Corps and prevent it from moving north. Similar attacks could be made against the German IInd Corps by the Czechs or an army from the Carpathian district and perhaps an air assault division employed in the mountains.

Frontal Aviation would achieve a sortie rate of three to four per aircraft per day, a total of over 2,000 ground attack sorties on forward NATO forces. The Aviation Armies' 24th Air Army Su-24 'Fencers' would fly deep raiding missions against key reinforcement points. Their targets could include air trooping centres from Hanover and Frankfurt in Germany to Mildenhall in England. Military ports in the Low Countries would also be attacked as would the huge warehouses near Kaiserslautern which contain much of the US Army's pre-positioned equipment for forces flying in from the continental US. Aviation and special forces would also be engaged in a struggle to knock out NATO nuclear delivery-means aircraft, missiles, heavy guns, etc.

If the Pact forces were able to sustain a rate of advance of say 35km per day they would reach the Netherlands in eight or nine days. This represents the worst case possible for NATO, and there are a number of reasons why it would probably not materialise. Soviet norms stipulating rates of advance are unrealistic in many scenarios. These figures of 35km per day are comparable to the major successes of the Red Army near the end of the war. But by the time of the Oder-Vistula and Berlin operations when such rates were achieved the Germans had completely lost control of the skies and much of their front line was composed of old men and schoolboys. The Red Army was able to mass crushing superiorities of 6:1 in tanks and artillery not just in breakthrough sectors but over the whole front. Today much of NATO's front line is composed of superb professional troops and its inferiority in tank numbers is compensated for by a superiority of anti-tank missiles and helicopters. Much of Germany is built up, and as recent events in Beirut have shown a determined defence of urban areas is possible even against well-trained armies. Even with a favourable initial balance of power brought about by a surprise strike the Soviet conquest

Above left:
Against NATO's well-equipped anti-tank forces the very large amount of armour in the Soviet order of battle could prove a liability. *via C. F. Foss*

Left:
Against an enemy heavily equipped with anti-tank systems the careful co-ordination of tanks, infantry and artillery is essential. *Novosti*

Right:
**The limits of mobility: a recovery
vehicle rescues a bogged tank —
even in the missile age, climate
and terrain can decide the
outcome of mechanised
operations.** *via C. F. Foss*

of Germany would take weeks not days.

A protracted conflict would allow the Soviets to bring another six or so armies into Europe and the Americans to implement their 'Return of Forces to Germany' plans. Together with German and British mobilisations NATO could add another dozen or so divisions, or division equivalents, to the order of battle. Ten days of heavy losses would see the Soviets relying on outdated T-55 and T-62 tanks and their Eastern allies on T-34s, but of course Western armies would also suffer from this attrition. Few analysts believe that the belligerents would fight to this stage of exhaustion, and that nuclear or chemical weapons might be used to break the impasse.

It is hard to imagine how the mobilisation of the three or four million men required to bring the Pact's forces to full mobilisation could ever be concealed, or indeed ignored by any Western politician. Such national mobilisation which would take three or four months would naturally allow NATO to call on its own reserves. With so many additional units available on each side the dispositions of troops would probably appear quite different to those set out in the limited mobilisation map. Although full mobilisation would give the Russians a distinct superiorty in numbers it would still seem insufficient for the lightning victory which their theorists believe is possible.

In all of these scenarios it would seem that only a large nuclear strike coupled with strategic surprise could guarantee a rapid Soviet victory. This is not to say that they could not achieve this without resort to large scale use of weapons of mass destruction but that their chances of doing so are distinctly limited. To be sure of success they need to decimate NATO's major field groupings with nuclear strikes, and there can be little doubt that Western commanders would then favour retaliation in kind. Some Soviet strategists write in a matter of fact way about neutralising NATO's nuclear retaliatory forces. Even if attacks by aviation, artillery, special forces and manoeuvre groups using conventional or nuclear munitions were extremely successful eliminating say 95% of the allies' tactical and theatre nuclear weapons there would still be enough left to completely devastate the Soviet Army — for stockpiles of just these warheads in Europe number 7,000. Evidently on the Central Front there is still an approximate balance of military power: practically speaking both sides would be unable to start a war in the certainty of winning it. The Soviet's best chance would lie in a partial mobilisation which did not alarm the West, followed by a surprise attack. Such offensive might bring about a victory in a few weeks if the Soviet Army performed superbly. But it is equally possible to imagine the calamities that might befall it. Lured into prepared killing zones, its heavily mechanised forces could be decimated by NATO armies saturated with modern anti-tank weapons. The demands of the Soviet theorists' high speed shock offensive might prove beyond the capabilities of the low level commanders, and would the Russian soldiers perform with the heroism that they exhibited against the Nazi's, under an all-powerful leader such as Stalin when their homeland had been invaded, in an aggressive war against the capitalists under today's leadership of ageing grey men in the Kremlin?

An assault in the north, against Norway, would see a heavier initial preponderance of Soviet power. Two motor rifle divisions, a marine regiment and an air assault division (totalling 30,000 combat troops) could be sent into action with very little strategic warning. A single Norwegian brigade would oppose them until reinforcements from the

Allied Command Mobile Force arrived: on paper at least it would seem that the Soviets could achieve a quick victory. But their advance would have to be conducted down a single road running hundreds of miles down the fjord-indented coastline. A determined defence of this road would force them to make continuous envelopments of the defending forces by air and sea landings, and they would need local air superiority for this. A Soviet strike might be aimed at vital intelligence gathering installations in northern Norway used for tracking Russian submarines and would make good headway, particularly if allied reinforcements had not arrived. Because of the favourable balance of strength, small local population, and geographical remoteness of northern Norway it would be a good target for a limited Soviet advance, or a retaliation for some loss to them elsewhere.

Operations in the Southwest European TVD might be directed against Greece, Turkey, Yugoslavia, Austria and Italy. The Soviet Army's only forward-based combat-ready forces available for such an action would be the four divisions of the Southern Group of Forces. A war against Greece or Turkey would require major troop movements of units drawn from the Odessa and Kiev districts. Travel across Rumania to the front line would depend on the goodwill of the Bucharest government, as for some years it has refused to have Soviet troops on its soil. Concentration of a big enough army to wage war on Greece would be difficult without losing the factor of surprise. The Greeks have large ground forces (150,000 soldiers organised into 14 divisions and three corps) which although poorly equipped hold good positions in the so-called 'Macedonian Line' fortifications on the Greco-Bulgarian frontier. A Pact attack on the Greeks would aim to exploit a number of river valleys (the Vardar, Struma and Nestos) which run south to the Aegean. An operation against the Turkish part of the Balkans would aim to use the plain of the Ergene river to allow a rapid advance on the Dardanelles. The Bulgarians would be keen to join a military venture against the Turks and might provide two of their armies.

The Southern Group might also be used to attack southern Germany via the Danube

Above left:
Two motor rifle divisions could be committed against Norway with very little strategic warning.
Novosti

Below left:
Geography would force the Russians to envelop a defensive force in northern Norway continuously by both air and sea. The 76th Guards Air Assault Division might well be assigned to the Northern TVD for such landings. *Novosti*

Below:
Ski-borne special forces could infiltrate northern Norway ahead of the main force. *Novosti*

corridor but this assumes either Austrian acquiescence or a war against them. Similarly Yugoslavian co-operation would be needed for offensive actions against Italy. Short of a general war there is always the possibility that the forces of the Southwestern theatre might be used for a Czech-style police action against Rumania should the leadership in Bucharest become too independently minded, or perhaps against Yugoslavia should a power vacuum occur there. Rumania represents a remarkable example of a Warsaw Pact state which has actually trained its forces more or less overtly in a doctrine of territorial defence designed to resist a Russian intervention. How successful such a defence would be we simply cannot tell.

The paucity of combat-ready forward-based Russian forces, the long line of communication across often difficult terrain, and the existence of a bloc of neutral states (Yugoslavia, Austria, and to a lesser degree Rumania) would all hinder a surprise action by the Pact in the Southwestern TVD. With preparation they could launch an offensive against NATO's Balkan southern flank, but with limited chances given the large size of Greece and Turkey's forces.

War in the South

The Southern Theatre of Military Operations embraces the Transcaucasus, North Caucasus, Turkestan, and possibly Central Asian districts and the forces in Afghanistan. They might be used in a war against Turkey, or one in the Middle East.

The largest concentration of divisions is in the Transcaucasus MD, but their readiness is so low (three category II, and eight category III) that a surprise attack on Turkey would seem to be out of the question. They would have to mobilise 78,000 men (25% of the strength of three divisions and 75% of eight) to bring the line divisions up to strength, at least 100,000 of one includes support units. If the forces of the North Caucasus district were made up to strength and moved south another seven divisions (five MR, one Tk and one Arty) could be thrown into the battle. The combined total of around 210,000 combat troops (which would take a couple of months to mobilise and move south) would then take on a Turkish Army whose peace-time standing strength is 470,000. Even if the majority of Turkey's 10 corps (consisting of 16 divisions and 19 separate brigades) were wiped out in a preliminary conventional or nuclear strike the Soviet Army would still have to fight a defender of equal strength holding fortified positions in mountains. Soviet supplies would be dependent on three railway lines (in places single-track) through the Caucasus mountains. For all of these reasons a Russian offensive against the Turks is a non-starter. Although naval deployments of the Black Sea Fleet in the eastern Mediterranean constitute a danger to

Right:
Forces from the Kiev district would provide an armoured exploitation force for operations in southwestern Europe. *Novosti*

Below right:
Hungarian T-55As breach a minefield with mine ploughs. Hungary's forces would be committed to the Southwest European TVD. *ADN*

NATO a simple comparison of strengths and study of the terrain reveals that there is no land threat to the southern flank. Indeed a comparison of the peacetime strengths of the Transcaucasus district (around 60,000 Ground Forces) and the Turkish Army reveals to a Kremlin politican a threat to the USSR.

An increasingly important scenario is that of a Soviet drive towards the oilfields of the Persian Gulf. The only major Gulf oil producer that borders the USSR is Iran. The forces available for an attack on the Iranians would include those in the North Caucasus, Turkestan and Transcaucasus districts and those in Afghanistan. Estimates of Iranian military strength are vague but it is believed that around 150,000 serve in the army and a similar number in the Revolutionary Guards, most of whom are currently fighting the Iraqi Army in the long running Gulf War. Certainly the Russians could brush aside the small units that have remained to guard the frontier, and important targets in depth could be seized by air assault forces after the rapid attainment of air superiority. But unlike Europe, key objectives in the Middle East are hundreds of miles from the Soviet start line. The Gulf War which began with an Iraqi assault with heavily mechanised forces organised and equipped along Soviet lines teaches some important lessons. The Iraqis, over the large areas of the front, were unable to achieve in three years of fighting the 35km advances which according to Soviet doctrine they should have achieved in the first 24 hours. Much of the fighting on the Iranian side has been done by hastily trained Revolutionary Guards, and the mullahs have quite a reserve of martyrs to call on in a nation of 39million people. Even if the Russians reached the oilfields they would have to defend lines of communication over 750 miles long against guerillas.

An attempt to take oilfields in a country not bordering the USSR would meet with greater problems. Firstly, deployment would have to be by air and sea. A corps of three air assault divisions (with support elements around 27,000 men) would take about two weeks to deploy to an airhead in the Gulf. But this could only be achieved if the entire serviceable strength of military Transport Aviation would be available and could

Left:
A push south, to the oilfields of the Persian Gulf, would take the Soviet Army across hundreds of miles of inhospitable terrain.
Novosti

Below:
BM-21 katyushas about to open fire. These weapons are grouped into army-level regiments.
Novosti

The Naval Landing

Although Soviet amphibious forces remain small they have an important role to play, particularly in the Baltic area.

Below:
H–Hour. The first assault wave is carried ashore by hovercraft. Hovercraft like this 'Aist' class vessel can pass over mines and underwater obstacles safely. *ADN*

Below right:
H+45 minutes. BTR-60s take to the water from their landing ship. *ADN*

Bottom:
H+1. The beach secured, landing ships beach, disgorging reinforcements. *Novosti*

Bottom right:
H+5. The armour has pushed inland to beat off a counter-attack. The Naval Infantry have fulfilled their mission and regular troops take over the advance. *Novosti*

overfly neutral or hostile countries. The Soviet ability to project power beyond countries on its borders remains limited. Although it possesses a large airborne arm, airlift capacity is limited, and there are only modest amphibious forces. It would be unable to land a force of naval infantry larger than regimental strength in the Gulf at the time of writing. Certainly the Soviets would be able to use their projection forces to take advantage of a collapse of authority in some far-away country, but are unable to conduct these operations against major opposition.

War in the East

It is difficult to imagine just what series of events would cause the Soviet Union to take military action against the People's Republic of China. Surely it would never willingly wage war on this nation of 1,000million people. Two general scenarios are possible: a war from a standing start, and one with a full mobilisation. From the point of the existing military balance a war with available forces would favour the Chinese. The Transbaikal, Siberian and Far Eastern districts and forces in Mongolia between them contain six tank and 37 motor rifle divisions, of which approximately half of the latter are cadre formations. Chinese forces in the northeastern and northern military regions have 46 main force infantry (and 29 local force) divisions and eight tank divisions.

The only strategy that would guarantee success over these forces in Manchuria would involve the widespread use of weapons of mass destruction. A large scale first strike would stand a good chance of completely disabling the modest Chinese nuclear strategic forces. Nuclear bursts and chemical weapons could then be used to reduce land forces to manageable strengths. The ground offensive could follow closely the 1945 offensive waged against the Japanese (depicted in

chapter one). Indeed current dispositions show a number of tank formations poised to repeat the feat of 6th Guards Tank Army in 1945. They would need to mobilise their reserves in the Far East to do this, and the experience of the last war shows us that this could take months. Filling out category II and III units in the Far Eastern TVD would require around 170,000 men, or 250,000 including support elements. Because the local population is so sparse in the Siberian and Transbaikal districts many of these men would have to be brought from European Russia. If the Far Eastern theatre was the only front on which they were fighting further divisions (perhaps 10) could be brought down the Trans-Siberian Railway from the Ural, Moscow, Leningrad and Volga districts. Liberal use of nuclear and chemical strikes might allow the Soviets to repeat the success of their last Manchurian offensive, but to what end? What would the aims of an aggressive war against China be? Even if it succeeded in taking northeastern China quickly it is unlikely that the loss of this strategic sector would in itself mean the defeat of the whole Chinese people.

On the other hand the current balance of forces does favour the Chinese significantly. Unmobilised the line divisions of the Far Eastern theatre contain around 250,000 combat troops with perhaps another 100,000 in support, but the Chinese People's Liberation Army strength in the north and northeastern regions is estimated at 1½million troops. There is the possibility that the Soviets might be forced to assume the strategic defensive in the Far East. During the late 1960s and early 1970s there were a number of border clashes between these two communist giants, and these were exploited by the Peking regime to whip up sympathy abroad and anti-Russian hysteria at home. The border clashes took place during the Chinese Cultural Revolution, and in this atmosphere of political turmoil there were fears in Moscow that Chinese military provocation might draw the Soviet Union into a war. The build-up of forces was begun and the Soviets even emplaced hundreds of old tank turrets around their cities in the region. The modernisation of the air assault divisions was accelerated so that they could be used to reinforce weak sectors on the long border quickly.

The political climate in Peking has stabilised since the days of the Cultural Revolution, but the Chinese are still pursuing their territorial dispute with the Russians, claiming large areas of mineral-rich eastern Siberia. An attack by them could quickly capture Soviet cities like Khabarovsk and Vladivostock which are situated close to the border. Balanced against the numerical superiority of the Chinese troops is the fact that they are largely unmechanised and would only be able to sustain a slow advance into Siberia. Although the equipment of the Soviet eastern garrison is obsolete by the standards of the Central European Front it is still superior to that of the Chinese forces. Although the two states compete for influence in the Pacific it is unlikely that the Chinese would find acceptable the risks of attacking Russia in pursuit of their territorial claims. Whilst China is the only state with conventional forces large enough to put the Russians on the strategic defensive it still lacks the nuclear forces needed to deter a retaliatory strike on its population centres.

The forces of the Far Eastern TVD might also be employed against Japan. Once again

Above:
Troops prepare to fire 'Scud' rockets. China's army is ill-equipped to withstand nuclear and chemical strikes.

Below:
An M-1946 130mm gun opens fire. The Chinese, in common with the Soviets, remain firm believers in the use of massed artillery.
Novosti

there is a territorial dispute over the Kunashiri, Etorofu, Shikotan and Habomai islands in the Kurile archipelago. These were taken from the Japanese in the wake of the defeat in 1945.

Since then Soviet and Japanese forces have occupied positions separated by the La Perouse strait which could in war become an important deployment route for vessels of the Pacific Fleet. The need to secure the strait might well necessitate a combined operation to seize the northern port of Hokkaido Island. Forces available for such an operation include 79 and 342 motor rifle divisions, a heliborne brigade, and headquarters 15th Army, all stationed on Sakhalin Island, and naval infantry from Vladivostock. Sufficient amphibious forces are available to land the two naval infantry regiments as a first echelon (and heliborne and air assault forces could be inserted at the same time) and then follow up with the motor rifle divisions. The principal problems facing such an operation would be the well prepared Japanese positions on Hokkaido, the Japanese Navy, and the presence of American nuclear strike aviation in Japan.

Four Paradoxes of Soviet Land Power

Although the Soviet Army must plan for war in all of these theatres with their very different geo-political characteristics it does so with a single military doctrine, a single system of command, and a single system of training and administration. These are perhaps four central elements of Soviet land power, four paradoxes, four themes which more than any others allow us to understand both the strengths and the weaknesses of the system.

The Offensive War

The commitment to an offensive war is the most important feature of Military Doctrine: it is a commitment rooted in the experience of the Great Patriotic War. Because the Germans were allowed to attack first, Russia suffered catastrophic loss of life and economic damage, and because the Red Army eventually adopted an offensive strategy far more effective than Hitler's blitzkrieg it won the greatest military victories (in terms of men and machines committed) in history. The retention of an offensive doctrine and sufficient forces to carry it out have been central elements of the Kremlin's postwar security policy. If the success or failure of that policy is judged in terms of keeping the Soviet Union safe from invasion then it has been a success. Today no Western leader would actually claim that Russia could be defeated by force of arms. But the paradox is that this security policy based on an offensive style of war only serves to generate insecurity in Russia's neighbours. The very doctrine which the marshals see as the central theme

Below:
Men of the Border Troops would be the first to resist any Chinese push into Siberia. *via C. F. Foss*

Below right:
Motor rifle troops on the move in Siberia. Signalling by flag is still commonly practised at troop level. *MoD*

Right:
SA-4 'Ganef' TELs move across open country. *Novosti*

114

The mass army needs a constant flow of manpower. Most NCOs are conscripts and there is a shortage of experienced cadre personnel. *Novosti*

Above right:
Soviet infantry in the assault. Traditionally the Russians have relied on shock and momentum rather than on the quality of their foot soldiers. *via C. F. Foss*

in their country's security is central to the insecurity of the West Germans, or the Chinese. The result is an arms race every bit as ruinous to the Soviets as it is to the West.

The Mass Army

Geography and Military Doctrine have left the Soviets with no other choice than to have a huge army. Soviet security policy requires enormous groups of armies to be permanently maintained. The need to expand these forces in wartime necessitates the maintenance of a large pool of trained reservists, all of which makes conscription the only way to fill the ranks. An enormous conscription, training and reserve system, has evolved to quench the mass army's thirst for manpower. Every year the Ground Forces alone mobilise around 700,000 conscripts and shed the same number of trained men.

Because of the size of the army and relatively short period of service expensive training exercises and aids simply are not affordable. The low allocations of rounds for gunnery training or track mileage for exercises with combat vehicles spoken of by Soviet emigres mean that the Soviet soldier is less well trained than his counterparts in a number of Western armies. Their training gives each man a basic grasp of his job in war and little more. This is not a new phenomenon; the strict adherence to drills made necessary by this unsophisticated training, and tendency for combat efficiency to fall markedly when the battle does not go to plan, are traits that have been observed by enemies from German generals on the Eastern Front to the Afghan mujahadeen.

Equipment Modernisation

A sizeable proportion of the Soviet economy is dedicated to producing defence hardware, and for the last few decades it has done so

very efficiently. The idea that Soviet weapons have only recently begun to match weapons produced in the West in sophistication is a myth. Anybody who believes that the T-72 is the first Soviet tank to match Western technology should read the dispatches of those shaken German panzer commanders who first came face to face with T-34s and KV-1s. They have embraced many postwar advances in military technology but have also chosen to produce evolutionary and robust designs rather than indulge in some of the technological experimentation practised by some Western armies.

The Russians rarely lack the know-how, it is the high technology and massive industrial effort required to modernise rapidly the mass army in peacetime that are the problems. By the time sufficient T-54/5 tanks had been produced to replace the wartime T-34 the 'new' tank was itself quite obsolete. During the postwar years the qualitative gap between the equipment in high readiness units and in the low readiness cadre formations has grown steadily wider. All armies have problems modernising but few have one of these proportions: in the mid-1970s some units had received brand new T-72s whilst others in less important regions soldiered on with tanks built during the war. Imagine a British Army with Chieftain Mk 5s serving alongside Cromwells.

Clearly there are limits to the resources that the Soviets can devote to modernising their forces. New weapons are delivered constantly to the high-readiness forward-based units in an attempt to keep them on a technological par with NATO forces. But the price of constantly re-equipping the groups of forces and elements of the second strategic echelon in the western USSR is that many cadre units have been left with outdated hardware. The introduction of high technology, high cost systems such as the SA-8 in one division in East Germany means that several others in the Siberian or North Caucasus districts may have to retain S-60 anti-aircraft guns. During the Brezhnev era there was a steady growth in defence spending against a background of healthy economic growth, but today the economic growth rate is half of what it was in the 1960s. Further growth in defence spending will be financed at the expense of the rest of the economy, notably the consumer sector.

Command and Control

During the war Red Army leadership, particularly at the front level, was often outstanding. Both the Czechoslovak and Afghan operations have offered evidence that in terms of strategic command and staff work the marshals have not lost their touch. The General Staff, in effect the brain of the Soviet Army, works not only to implement decisions but also to formulate new doctrine, introduce new technology and educate the officer corps. The Staff and the key councils of military and political leadership are at the apex of the pyramid of command, a pyramid designed to allow the quickest and most efficient communication of orders downwards. This rigid centralisation of command and control is both a great strength at the strategic level and a great weakness at the tactical level.

The Russian attitude to command and control is well summed up by Lt-Gen V. Reznichenko: 'the success of offensive combat is directly dependent on the level of training of commanders and staffs: the lower that level the greater must be the degree of centralised control'. But to win the great victories and advance at the speed Soviet strategists believe is possible, brilliance is needed at all levels of command if a determined opposition is to be overcome. It is very difficult to expect this in an army where adherence to orders is constantly stressed and initiative stifled. It is asking a geat deal to expect outstanding leadership from an NCO corps in which very few sergeants have more than two years' military experience. It is precisely because of the weakness of its junior officers and NCOs that the Soviet Army's performance in rural operations in Afghanistan, on the rare occasions when it has attemped them, has been so mediocre.

Both the Warsaw Pact and NATO are experimenting with new military doctrines and weapons that may well lead to the breakdown of front lines and the inter-penetration of forces to a greater extent than ever before. These doctrines require greater initiative and panache on the part of junior commanders, and it remains to be seen how the Soviets will solve these demands.

Traditionally they have relied on mass and firepower to outweigh these weaknesses, so far with success for they have never suffered a major defeat. Indeed on the occasions when they have used their land power they have redrawn the map. It is all very well to speculate whether or not the Soviets would succeed in a war against western Europe or China, but, whether they won or not, a war against them would be an unspeakable catastrophe. Mistrust of the West and a fear that they might once again be the victims of an attack have fuelled the Russian military build-up. The route to peace and stability lies in the relaxation of tension rather than in the ceaseless acquisition of military power for its own sake. The vicious circle of insecurity which fuels the current arms build-up must be broken soon, but it must be done by statesmen before the military forces of East and West are called upon to go to war and redraw the map.

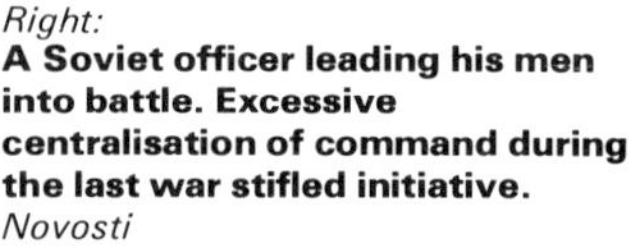

APPENDICES

East Germany
(All category I)

Military District III — HQ Liepzig

7 Tk Div	Dresden
11 MR Div	Halle
4 MR Div	Erfurt
Arty Regt	Liepzig

Military District V — HQ Neubrandenburgh

9 Tk Div	Eggesin
8 MR Div	Potsdam
1 MR Div	Schwerin
Arty Regt	Torgelow

Army level support also includes anti-aircraft and anti-aircraft missile regiments, engineer, chemical warfare, signals and transport battalions.

Internal Security: 48,000 Border Troops; 16,000 Alert Police and 5,000 Ministry of State Security troops.

Also available are two engineer regiments, two airborne special forces battalions, and a signals regiment.

Hungary

Western Military District HQ Szekesfehervar

5 Tk Div (cat II)	Tatabanya
9 MR Div (cat II)	Szombathely
12 MR Div (cat II)	Dombovar

Eastern Military District HQ Szolnok

4 MR Div (cat III)	Kecskemet
17 MR Div (cat III)	Salgotajan
27 MR Div (cat III)	Debrecen

Support includes three artillery regiments, one 'Scud' missile brigade, two air defence missile regiments, one air defence artillery regiment, and an airborne battalion.

Internal Security: 15,000 Internal Security Troops and 15,000 Frontier Guards.

Poland

Pomeranian Military District

	HQ Bydgoszcz
16 Tk Div (cat I)	Elblag
20 Tk Div (cat I)	Szczecinek
12 MR Div (cat I)	Szczecin
8 MR Div (cat I)	Koszalin
15 MR Div (cat I)	Olsztyn
7 Amphib Asslt Div (cat II)	Gdansk
6 Arty Bde	Torun

Silesian Military District — HQ Wroclaw

5 TK Div (cat I)	Gubin
10 Tk Div (cat I)	Opote
11 Tk Div (cat I)	Zagan
2 MR Div (cat II) 'Henrik Dombrovski'	Nysa
4 MR Div (cat II)	Krosno-Odryanskie
5 Arty Bde	Glogow

Warsaw Military District — HQ Warsaw

1 MR Div (cat III) 'Tadeusz Kosciuszko'	Lebignovo
3 MR Div (cat III) 'Ramuald Traugutt'	Lublin
9 MR Div (cat III)	Rzeszow
6 Air Asslt Div (cat I) 'Pommorska'	Cracow
1 Arty Bde	Wegorzovo

There are also four 'Scud' brigades, three special forces brigades, five anti-aircraft artillery regiments, three anti-tank regiments and a SA-4 brigade. Each MD would become an army in war.

Internal Security: 56,000 Internal Security and 16,000 Border Troops.

Czechoslovakia

1st Army (Western Military
District) HQ Tabor
4th Army (Eastern Military District)
HQ Trencin

1 Tk Div (cat I)	Pilzen
4 Tk Div (cat II)	Bratislava
9 Tk Div (cat II)	Pilzen
13 Tk Div (cat III)	Trencin
14 Tk Div (cat III)	Presor
2 MR Div (cat I)	Karlovy-Vary
3 MR Div (cat II)	Pilzen
15 MR Div (cat III)	Bratislava
19 MR Div (cat III)	Jillava
20 MR Div (cat III)	Brno
22 Air Asslt Bde	Porznitz

The two army HQs have an artillery regiment, 'Scud' missile brigade, and anti-aircraft regiment each at their disposal. A third 'Scud' brigade is under central control.

Internal Security: 11,000 Border Troops.

Bulgaria

1st Army	HQ Sofia
1 Gds MR Div (cat III)	Sofia
28 MR Div (cat I or II)	Blagoevgrad
9 Tk Bde	Knyazhevo
? 'Scud' Bde	Samokov
2nd Army	HQ Plovdiv
2 MR Div (cat I or II)	Stara Zagora
17 MR Div (cat I or II)	Khaskovo
19 MR Div (cat III)	Pazardzhik
5 Tk Bde	Kazanluk
11 Tk Bde	Karlovo
? 'Scud' Bde	Karlovo
3rd Army	HQ Sliven
3 MR Div (cat I or II)	Burgas
7 MR Div (cat I or II)	Yambol
18 MR Div (cat III)	Shumen
13 Tk Bde	Sliven
24 Tk Bde	Aytos
? 'Scud' Bde	Yambol
? Air Asslt Regt	Burgas

Other troops include: four artillery regiments, four anti-aircraft artillery regiments, two reconnaissance battalions, and one mountain battalion. There are coastal artillery regiments under naval control.

Internal Security: 16,000 Border Guards and 7,500 Security Police.

Rumania

1st Army	HQ Bucharest
2nd Army	HQ Bacau
3rd Army	HQ Craiova
4th Army	HQ Cluj
4 Tk Div (cat II)	Bucharest
6 Tk Div (cat I)	Turgu Mures
10 MR Div (cat I ?)	Iasi
81 MR Div (cat III)	Bacau
? MR Div (cat II)	Braila
2 MR Div (cat III)	Craiova
1 MR Div (cat III)	Bucharest
11 MR Div (cat II)	Oradea
18 MR Div (cat II)	Timisuara
? MR Div (cat III)	Lugoj

Army troops include: three mountain regiments, three artillery regiments, two artillery brigades, two anti-aircraft artillery brigades, five anti-tank regiments, and an air assault regiment.

Internal Security: 17,000 Border Troops and 20,000 Security Troops.

Below:
NGF. Polish tanks of the Silesian Tank Army. It is possible that one of the Northern Group's tank divisions might be placed under the control of this HQ. *ADN*

BIBLIOGRAPHY

Soviet Sources (in Russian)

Belikov, V. A.: *Krasnoznamenniy Prikarpatskiy*; Voenizdat 1982.

Salmanov, G. I.: *Ordena Lenina Zabaikalskiy;* Voenizdat 1980.

Skrelnika, A. I.: *Zapad-81*; Voenizdat 1982.

(Various): *Istoriya Belikoi Otechestvennoi Voiny Sovetsko Soyuza*; Voenizdat 1961.

(Various): *Voyenni Entsiclopedechskiy Slovai*; Voenizdat 1983.

Krasnaya Zvevda (Red Star), Ministry of Defence daily paper.

Soviet Sources (in English)

Abyzov, V.: *The Final Assault*; Progress 1980.

Byely, B.: *Marxism-Leninism on War and Army* (translated by the United States Air Force); 1972.

Chuikov, V. I.: *The End of the Third Reich*; Panther 1969.

Grechko, A. A.: *The Armed Forces of the Soviet State*; Progress 1977.

Milovidov, A. S.: *The Philosophical Heritage of V. I. Lenin and Problems of Contemporary War*; (USAF) 1972.

Savkin, V. Ye.: *The Basic Principles of Operational Art and Tactics*; (USAF translation) 1972.

Shtemenko, S. M.: *The Soviet General Staff at War 1941-5*; Progress 1970.

Sidorenko, A. A.: *The Offensive*; (USAF translation) 1970.

Sokolovskiy, V. D.: *Military Strategy*; (USAF translation) 1970.

(Various): *Selected Readings from Military Thought 1963-1973*; (USAF translation) 1982.

(Various): *Whence the Threat to Peace*; Voenizdat 1982.

Soviet Military Review, published monthly by the Krasnaya Zvevda publishing house.

Other Books and Pamphlets

Central Intelligence Agency: *Directory of USSR Ministry of Defence and Armed Forces Officials*; National Foreign Assessment Centre 1982.

Central Intelligence Agency: *Status of Railroads in the USSR 1 April 1976*; 1976.

Defense Intelligence Agency: *Soviet Divisional Organizational Guide*; 1982.

Defense Intelligence Agency: *Physical Training of the Soviet Soldier*; 1982.

Defense Intelligence Agency: *Warsaw Pact Ground Forces Equipment Handbook*; 1980.

Department of Defense (USA):

Department of Defense: *Report to the Secretary of Defense FY 1978 Budget Request*.

Dawisha, K. and Hanson, P. (Eds): *East Military Power*; 1981, 1983 and 1984 editions.
Border Disputes; New English Library 1980.

Dinerstein, H. S.: *War and the Soviet Union*; Praeger 1959.

Erickson, J.: *The Soviet High Command*; MacMillan 1962.

Erickson, J.: *The Road to Berlin*; Weidenfeld 1983.

Fewtrell, D.: *The Soviet Economic Crisis: Prospects for the Military and the Consumer*; IISS 1983.

Forster, T. M.: *The East German Army*; George Allen and Unwin 1980.

Foss, C. F.: *Jane's Armour and Artillery 1983-84*; Jane's 1983.

Heikal, M.: *Sphinx and Commissar*; Collins 1978.

Garthoff, R. L.: *Soviet Military Doctrine*; Free Press 1954.

Hemsley, J.: *Soviet Troop Control*; Brassey's 1982.

Isby, D. C.: *Weapons and Tactics of the Soviet Army*; Jane's 1981.

International Institute of Strategic Studies: *The Military Balance 1983-4*; IISS 1983.

Kolkowicz, R.: *The Soviet Military and the Communist Party*; Princeton 1967.

Lewis, W. J.: *The Warsaw Pact — Arms Doctrine and Strategy*; McGraw Hill 1982.

Littell, R. (Ed): *The Czech Black Book*; Pall Mall Press 1969.

Jones, C. D.: *Soviet Influence in Eastern Europe*; Praeger 1981.

Mayer, S. L. (Ed): *The Soviet War Machine 1917-45*; Arms and Armour 1977.

OKH — Fremde Heere Ost, Truppen-Ubersicht und Kriegsliederungen Rote Armee; 1944.

Ross Johnson, A. (et al): *East European Military Establishments: The Warsaw Pact Northern Tier*; Rand 1980.

Schapiro, L.: *The Government and Politics of the Soviet Union*; Hutchinson 1979 Ed.

Suvorov, V.: *The Liberators*; Hamish Hamilton 1981.

Thompson, R. (Ed): *War in Peace*; Orbis 1981.

US Army Armor Center: *Soviet Tank Maintenance and Drivers Training*; Republished 1982.

US Army Armor Center: *Soviet Tank Gunnery*; Re-published 1982.

US Army Armor Center: *Soviet Tank Rail Transport*; Re-published 1982.

US Army Armor Center: *Organization and Equipment of the Soviet Army*; 1981.

US Army Intelligence and Security Command: *Soviet Army Operations*; 1978.

Vernon, G. V.: *Soviet Perceptions of War and Peace*; NDU Press 1981.

Vigor, P. H.: *The Soviet View of War, Peace and Neutrality*; Routledge and Keegan Paul 1975.

Vigor, P. H. (et al): *The Soviet War Machine*; Salamander 1980.

Vanderveen, B.: *Observers Military Vehicle Directory*; Warne 1972.

Zaloga, S. J.: *Modern Soviet Armour*; Arms and Armour 1979.

Periodicals

Armed Forces, published monthly by Ian Allan Ltd.

Armor, published monthly by the US Army Armor School.

Air Force Journal, published monthly by the Air Force Association.

Aviation Week and Space Technology, published weekly.

Defence, published monthly by the Whitton Press.

Defence Update International, published monthly by Eshel-Dramit.

Jane's Defence Review, published monthly, as of January 1984 weekly, by Jane's.

International Defence Review, published monthly by Interavia.

International Security, published monthly in Washington.

Problems of Communism, published monthly by US Information Agency.

RUSI Journal, published monthly by the Royal United Services Institute.

Survival, published monthly by the International Institute of Strategic Studies.

Machines like these Mil-24 'Hind-D' gunships could protect manoeuvre groups fighting deep in the NATO rear by flying anti-helicopter as well as anti-tank missions. *Novosti*